UNAFRAID TO BE

RUTH ETCHELLS

UNAFRAID TO BE

A Christian study of contemporary
English writing

87

INTER-VARSITY PRESS

INTER-VARSITY PRESS

Inter-Varsity Fellowship
39 Bedford Square, London WC1B 3EY

Inter-Varsity Press
Box F, Downers Grove, Illinois 60515

First Edition August 1969
Reprinted February 1972

ISBN 0 85110 344 8

Library of Congress Catalog Number 79-98156

Printed and bound in England by
Hazell Watson & Viney Ltd.
Aylesbury, Bucks

CONTENTS

ACKNOWLEDGMENTS

For permission to use copyright material, acknowledgment is made to the following: Abelard-Schuman Ltd for lines from 'The North' by Brian Higgins (in *The Only Need*); Jonathan Cape Ltd for lines from 'Fifteen Million Plastic Bags' by Adrian Mitchell (in *Poems*); Jonathan Cape Ltd and Random House, Inc. for quotations from *Chips with Everything* by Arnold Wesker; Faber and Faber Ltd and Random House, Inc. for lines from 'Song' by Stephen Spender (in *Collected Poems 1928–1953*); The Faith Press Ltd for 'To a dignitary who spoke contemptuously of a saint' (in *Pi in the High*); Rupert Hart-Davis for 'Schoonermen' by R. S. Thomas (in *Pieta*); David Higham Associates Ltd for lines from 'Apocalypse' by D. J. Enright (published by Chatto and Windus Ltd in *Addictions*); Laurie Lee for 'April Rise' (published by John Lehmann Ltd in *The Bloom of Candles*); Christopher Logue for lines from 'The Song of the Dead Soldier' (published by Faber and Faber Ltd in *Songs*); Macmillan and Co. Ltd, London, the Macmillan Company of Canada and St Martin's Press, Inc. for lines from 'A Song about Major Eatherly' by John Wain (in *Weep before God*), and lines from 'Kew Bridge' by Zulfikar Ghose (in *Jets from Orange*); Routledge and Kegan Paul Ltd for lines from 'The Archaeologist' by Peter Redgrove (in *The Collector and Other Poems*); SCM Press Ltd for quotations from *Letters and Papers from Prison* by Dietrich Bonhoeffer; Southern Music Publishing Company Ltd for lines from 'The Universal Soldier' by Buffy Sainte-Marie; Thames and Hudson Ltd and the University of Indiana Press for 'Sonnet' by Miguel de Guavera (in *Anthology of Mexican Poetry*).

King Christ, this world is all aleak;
and life-preservers there are none:
and waves which only He may walk
Who dares to call Himself a man.

E. E. CUMMINGS

PREFACE

I think the best way to explain what this book is supposed to be is to make quite clear initially what it is not. It is not, for instance, either literary criticism or literary history. It does not evaluate in literary terms today's writing, nor catalogue exhaustively (nor even summarize) the mass of poetry, drama and novels of the last fifteen years. Nor, on the other hand, is it about the theory behind the Christian's encounter with contemporary culture. It does not analyse the nature of art, the quality of the creative impulse, and the Christian participation in it. These are important questions which others have dealt with elsewhere.[1]

What the book does attempt to show is a possible Christian approach to contemporary writing. This is not *the* Christian view of literature; there is no such thing, and it is dangerous, because artificially limiting, to suggest that there is. It is a particular approach by an individual Christian, based on the belief that, while there is no one Christian manner of encountering literature, there is, or should be, in the approach of Christians to the culture of their age a common denominator which is demonstrably Christian.

Since example is better than precept, perhaps the most satis-

[1] See, *e.g.*, George Every, *Poetry and Personal Responsibility* (SCM, 1949); Valerie Pitt, *The Writer and the Modern World* (SPCK, 1966); S. B. Babbage, *The Mark of Cain* (Paternoster, 1966); Donald Whittle, *Christianity and the Arts* (Mowbray, 1966); Derek Kidner, *The Christian and the Arts* (IVP, 1959); *London Quarterly and Holborn Review*, October 1965.

factory way to suggest it is actually to do it. So the pages that follow are really a Christian exposition of one person's encounter with recent literature. It is a study of what modern writers are writing about, and what I, as a Christian, find my response to them to be. As such I have found it of great personal value. If others, in sharing the reactions and ponderings of the pages that follow, find themselves stimulated to weigh and establish their own judgments and responses, and to examine honestly, without prejudice or position-defending, the relevance of the Christian faith to what today's authors are so urgently expressing, then the exercise will have been doubly worth while.

1 'CLIFFS OF FALL'
An introduction

O the mind, mind has mountains; cliffs of fall
Frightful, sheer, no-man-fathomed. Hold them cheap
May who ne'er hung there.[1]

Mountains are like that. You do not need to have swung on the
rock face with dizzy space between your boots to know that
extraordinarily mixed sensation—half joy, half fear—that is the
average human being's response to an encounter with the hills.
For many of us just to see them is enough. Somehow they bring
to the surface our knowledge of our own selves as human beings,
our awareness that in all things, including our maturing as people,
what is a potential height can also be a potential depth. We sense
that this challenge to achievement is also a threat of crash, that
vision and light are here, but the reverse, darkness and despair,
seem just as possible. And so, because it reflects what we glimpse
of ourselves, in the image of the mountain we recognize at once a
hope and a doubt within.

It is with this visionary hope and this profound doubt about
ourselves that contemporary English literature is concerned. Of the
many charges which are made against modern writing, triviality is
not one that may be sustained; for present-day authors are involved
in examining, implicitly or explicitly, a wide range of human
thought and values. Inevitably, therefore, they hang on the 'cliffs
of fall' of which G. M. Hopkins spoke in the lines quoted above,

[1] From G. M. Hopkins, 'No worst, there is none', *Poems of Gerard
Manley Hopkins*[3] (OUP, 1948).

those sheer mountains of the mind and spirit where security seems a dream and disaster a near certainty. Encounter with such writing involves encounter not only with vision but with nightmare, for in view of the present-day ruthless blasting away of all human presuppositions, no-one can avoid facing the ultimate horror, as well as the ultimate hope, possible for the human race.

THE NECESSITY OF CULTURE

In view of this, it is essential to ask whether the reading of modern fiction or the appraising of modern drama is a proper study for any student unless they form part of the course which he is taking. Why should the geologist or chemist, the geographer, musician or physicist concern himself with such matters? This is an urgent contemporary question, for much of the current debate about the role of a university or of higher education generally is directly related to it. As students we use our minds to grapple with the intellectual challenges of our particular academic discipline. But recent upheavals would underline that we do not properly stop there, that our task involves more than using our brain only on our own subject.

There are still many who would argue that this is not so. Their reason for being members of a college or university is solely to become linguists or chemists, more knowledgeable classicists or engineers. They have neither time nor inclination for studying anything which does not bear on this. But there is a serious danger in such an attitude which may not lightly be disregarded. C. P. Snow clarified it some years ago in his concern that scientists should not live islanded, since they are essentially part of the community and cannot therefore opt out of the responsibility for their effect upon it. His point is valid for all specialist groups who by training or choice are cut off from, or are ignorant of, the needs and tensions and pressures of the society in which they live. To be so is to disregard a fundamental aspect of human nature; membership of the corporate human race is inescapable, and therefore, however desirable it may seem to pursue one's study in isolation, it cannot be done.

If we cannot escape our corporateness and its implications for our studies, neither can we escape the complexity of our individual personalities. No human being is reducible to a single aspect. George is not just a mathematician; George is also a man. As a man he is linked with other people and varied interests—parents, girlfriend, football team, newsagent, local MP, and even, perhaps, the local parson. All these add something to George the mathematician to make George the man. And if he is fully to be a man, he must learn to apply the same cogency he uses in his specialist academic studies to the culture of his age, and to the many physical, emotional, rational and spiritual problems, both individual and social, which that culture reflects.

A student or scholar who rejects this may well suffer from the insidious disease of perpetually 'narrow-fronted' maturity. Unless he is prepared to use his mind on matters outside his particular subject with the energy and integrity he applies to that subject, he denies himself the possibility of multi-directional growth, because he is denying the relevance of his study to himself as a whole person, to the age in which he lives, and to mankind generally. For the mathematician, for instance, is not a brain in a vacuum: he is a being whose delicate awareness of himself and other beings demands the same sensitivity, accuracy and probity as his nicest mathematical calculation.[2]

GRIEF AND GLORY

It is because these qualities of sensitivity, accuracy and probity are demanded that we all need to know what writers are saying in our age: writers, that is, not only of the editorials or the weeklies which neatly dehydrate the last seven days and present them to us canned and hygienic, but novelists and dramatists and poets who are able to capture the vitality, even the explosiveness, of the world in which they live, and make us aware of it too.

[2] At a course on modern literary criticism, sponsored by the Government Department of Education and Science in March 1965, Professor L. C. Knights insisted that thinking was the activity of the whole person: personal feelings and affections, moral integrity and thought and reason are co-influential. Deep thinking is therefore possible only to the deep feeler: poetic accuracy only to the man of veracity.

That brings us back to the danger we noted at the beginning, that a potential height is also a potential depth. The heights of vision implicit for us in many of today's writers are also potentially horrors of understanding. We may learn more of our human state than we are prepared to accept or face. In fact, we might go further and suggest that writers of today often give a picture of the human race which we feel unable, rather than unwilling, to encounter.

It is here that the perspective of the Christian faith, from the standpoint of which this book is written, is specially relevant. It has a great deal to say about the darkness of spirit which pervades man's modern consciousness. It both accepts its reality and supplies a dynamic to meet the force of desperation in the contemporary world which is reflected in the power of much of its writing. It looks at man as he really is and as modern writers insist he is. BBC television produced a song series in 1968 called 'Grief and Glory', which summed up what writers seem to be saying:

Now the earth has put on cold
And the stars have rusted old,
And the man knows how they were made.
He has grief and glory inside him,
And he seeks someone to guide him,
And sings of a love unknown.

It is of this 'grief and glory' known by modern man, and the 'someone to guide him' whom he seeks, that the Christian faith speaks. We shall look in detail at this in the final chapter, but there are certain general implications of approaching modern literature in the context of Christian belief that we must touch on here.

WEIGHING WHAT THEY SAY

There is, first, the standard of judgment it implies. Reading what is written is only the beginning. When we read, we have to judge: we have to reject or accept, be stirred by or turn away from. We may not even have worked out on what basis we do this, or what criteria we use. Indeed, the popular tendency is to argue that criteria do not matter (for judgments have no universal significance), that all standards, whether aesthetic or moral, are merely subjective.

Any standards we adopt do, of course, depend on what view of life we hold. If, for instance, we understand the world as essentially chaotic and absurd, then this can (though it need not)[3] lead us to a rejection of pattern, order and form as essentials of any art. Similarly, since the Christian sees man as made in a particular way, functioning properly only in obedience to certain moral, physical and spiritual laws, this provides a framework which will affect his judgment.

We must be quite clear about this. Assessing literature in the perspective of Christianity does not mean rejecting as of no serious value any writing that is un-Christian and accepting uncritically whatever claims to express the Christian view. Indeed, much so-called 'Christian literature' is neither literature nor Christian, because of its cliché-ridden style, vagueness and muddle of thought, unctuousness of tone or piety of sentiment, all of which deny the vitality, vigour and purity which is implicit in the Christian understanding of art.

It is this last point we must note particularly. That same Christian understanding will be rigorous in its analysis of all writing, including the non-Christian and the anti-Christian, that claims to be serious. For the Christian faith insists that absolutes do exist, that moral standards are not just a matter of opinion, of arbitrary social choice, of subjectivity, but are part of the human response to the laws by which God has created the world, and man, and his society within the world. The sense of loneliness and pointlessness, the dominance of the erotic and violent, lack of communication, alienation, disintegration, all these are part of the contemporary consciousness. But when modern writers express them negatively or destructively, the validity of what they say or the means they use is still assessable in the context of such Christian absolutes.[4]

[3] Some writers who expound the Absurd, *e.g.* Camus and Sartre, impose a finely-controlled form on their work which develops from their view of man, in a world of chaos, imposing his own order on his immediate existence by an act of heroic 'authenticity'.

[4] *Cf.* T. S. Eliot, 'Literary criticism should be completed by criticism from a definite ethical and theological standpoint. In so far as in any age there is common agreement on ethical and theological matters, so far can literary criticism be substantive. In ages like our own, in which

So an integrity of writing is demanded by honest Christian thinking at least as astringent as formally academic standards would require. Christian critical assessment of writers demands, not that they express the Christian view of life, but that they do not pervert its moral laws, sentimentalize man himself, or deny or blur aspects of his being and so falsify.

BEARING THE BATTERING

Yet while our sense of the true and false in modern writing is sharpened in this Christian context, this does not necessarily enable us to support the emotional, moral and spiritual effect of it. Contemporary writing is very largely a study of man without God. One might ask, therefore, with surprise if one is not a Christian and concern if one is, whether a proper Christian commitment can allow one to venture into the dark world of God-rejection. This can be put in two ways: by non-Christians, the accusation that Christianity is a form of escapism, a hole in which to hide from the sharp realities of the world around; by Christians, a concern that their commitment should remain deep and firm, their obedience pure, and their growth in Christian maturity unstunted. These two sides of the same question can perhaps be approached most helpfully by looking at what Christ Himself said and did about meeting the world He lived in, with its beliefs and non-beliefs, hopes and hates and fears and loves. As He prayed for His followers before His death, He said:

> Now I am no more in the world, but they are in the world, and I am coming to thee . . . They are not of the world, even as I am not of the world. I do not pray that thou shouldst take them out of the world, but that thou shouldst keep them from evil. . . . As

---

there is no such common agreement, it is the more necessary for Christian readers to scrutinize their reading, especially of works of imagination, with explicit ethical and theological standards. The "greatness" of literature cannot be determined solely by literary standards; though we must remember that whether it is literature or not can be determined only by literary standards' (from *Religion and Literature* (Faber and Faber, 1934)). *Cf.* K. Tynan's *Curtains* (Longmans, 1961).

thou didst send me into the world, so I have sent them into the world . . . I do not pray for these only, but also for those who are to believe in me through their word . . . that the world may believe that thou hast sent me.[5]

In the world but not of it; in it very fully, with as much sensitivity and awareness of our fellow inhabitants as we are capable of; up to the neck in it, but not influenced by it. All this was Christ's prayer for His disciples, then and now, and the pattern of His life on earth. And the 'world' includes the world of thought. So the Christian has more, not less, reason to involve himself in an understanding of what modern writers are saying. His attitude is one of responsibility and concern.

How, then, do we cope with things that trouble us in today's writing? How do we remain open and aware, yet influenced for good, not evil? What positive response is possible?

One or two practical considerations may help us, to begin with. The first is to recognize the variableness of our competence; that is, that we vary from day to day in our ability to cope. There will be moments in our lives, often arising from physical or mental as well as spiritual causes, when, whatever our commitment or faith, it will be inadvisable for us to read certain books, see certain films, when the encounter is not one we should deliberately undertake. It is important that these times are recognized as merely phases which are to be treated with self-knowledge and humour. They should no more condition our total attitude to the question than a temporarily strained muscle should that of a footballer to whom his game is his profession.[6]

Secondly, we should realize that we vary from person to person. Books which hardly affect some readers will have a deeply disturbing effect on others; and this means, of course, that we must exercise great care in urging reading-matter on other people. To shatter them into a state of awareness may be dramatic and exciting, but not much use if it has been done so urgently that the individual is shocked into a state of complete disintegration. We must, there-

[5] John 17:11-21.
[6] There will, of course, be some books which are never advisable reading. See below, p. 18.

fore, be sensitive to other people's competence, as well as to our own.

Deeper than either of these considerations is the need to examine as truthfully as possible what it is in twentieth-century literature that we find disturbing. Is it, for instance, the author's material or his intentions? One of the key distinctions we must make is between those writers who are setting out to titillate the senses, to exploit a perverted delight in violence, lust and cruelty for their own sake, and those who present them as a necessary part of any serious appraisal of life as the twentieth century knows it. A Christian understanding of life rejects as having no possible aesthetic, moral or spiritual justification the study of eroticism and violence as such, and would therefore condemn it with vigour. But writers who include the horrifying and the spiritually anarchistic in their descriptions because they are attempting to evaluate what life is cannot be rejected in this way. We dare not dismiss writing that is thoughtful on the grounds that it deals with elements in life, either physical or spiritual, on which we would prefer not to dwell.

CLIFFS OF FALL

Yet even where the writer's intention is serious we may find ourselves, whether committed to Christian belief or not, deeply shaken. Our beliefs and values seem insidiously undermined, our imagination and emotion violated. This is being 'troubled' in a much deeper sense, in the profoundest possible sense. It is the understanding of, the involvement in, the horror of great darkness in which so many live.

And at this profound level Christian love does not attempt to escape or withdraw.[7] Christ Himself, under the pressure of temptation and His agony for the world, faced it all in the context of prayer, of Scripture, and of His vital, living fellowhip with His

[7] 'Jesus asked in Gethsemane, "Could you not watch with me one hour?".... Man is summoned to share in God's sufferings at the hands of a godless world. He must therefore really live in the godless world, without attempting to gloss over . . . its ungodliness . . .' (Dietrich Bonhoeffer, *Letters and Papers from Prison*, revised by Frank Clarke *et al.* (SCM, 1967)).

Father; faced it right through Gethsemane, trial, torture and execution. When a Christian finds himself sharing this experience through his encounter with today's world, he can and must face it in this perspective of Christ's proven and continuous love for us, His Spirit's presence, God's concern for the whole world and His power to keep those who have trusted Him.

This is the most important implication of approaching modern writing in the context of Christian belief. Any tension we feel is no more than an acute form of a tension we know throughout our Christian lives. For we share the joys and agonies of the whole human race. We rejoice in a world God has made, exploring the gifts of creativity and imagination with which He has endowed us. But we realize, perhaps for the first time through the pages of contemporary literature, something of the loneliness and loss of twentieth-century man in a world which has largely rejected God. Inevitably there is a tension between our involvement in our common humanity and our involvement in our new humanity, that 'new creation' which is Christ's; between our continuing awareness of human failure and despair and our consciousness of divine victory on humanity's behalf. But we cannot run away from this tension. It will be with us as long as we live, and is part of our growing.

For the problem is deeper than the question of our own involvement. Today's man is making a journey into a strange and dark spiritual world where his voice echoes weirdly across chasms that seem unbridgeable and down gulfs which drop terrifyingly below him. As the effectiveness of education spreads, so more and more people will find themselves at least glimpsing these alien lands of the spirit: and many will make—indeed are making—the journey into these mountains of the mind, and are, perhaps, hopelessly scrambling amongst a diversity of paths. For these, the Christian message has something to say that is urgent and relevant.[8] But no Christian can say it if he does not know the problem:[9] and so more

[8] This is explored much more fully in the last section of this book.

[9] Moreover, he has a great deal to learn himself through encountering the problem. John Milton wrote, 'I cannot praise a fugitive and cloistered virtue ... that never sallies out' (*Areopagitica*, 1644).

must be prepared to venture among these 'cliffs of fall' because these cliffs are the world of twentieth-century man.

Of course it involves dangers. He is no honest mountaineer who 'conquers' the mountain by surveying the peak from a distance and then returns home to tell his friends how high it was and what were its perils. So the student particularly, if he is honest and committed, has to face up to the task of thinking through the ultimate question with which the literature of his day, the world of his generation, faces him. He has to do this because his calling as a student, and for some a calling as a Christian, demand of him not retreat from the society in which he lives but encounter within it. This book is concerned with some of the questions with which that encounter will face him, and with a possible approach to them.

2 A COMMON CONCERN
The contemporary theme

Most of us have taken part, and still do take part, and irritatedly hear other people take part, in the type of conversation that goes, 'You remember that accident we saw on Tuesday. . . .' 'No, it was Wednesday, because it was the day after Mrs Jones called.' 'No; it happened as we were coming down the hill after we'd found the shop shut, so it must have been early closing day, and that's Thursday . . .' And so on, and so on, sweetly reasonable and yet increasingly urgent, because in some irrational way the irrelevant details of time and place matter frightfully. They have come, in some way we do not analyse, to be identified with ourselves as we project those selves into the trivial incident we relate.

There is a similar experience common to most of us which is visual. We may have been quite small the first time it happened, and from time to time it may still occur. We catch sight of ourselves in the mirror and pause to stare; for a moment we are utterly alien from, and yet frighteningly involved in, the creature facing us. It is an unassessable and incalculable spirit which gazes back at us from the distancing glass. As we stare at it our private identity flickers and vanishes, meaningless before that inscrutability; and if we indulge the experience too long, our grasp on identity as an essential attribute of the human being is loosened and the mind and emotions swirl. Our touch, hesitant on the cold glass, seems our only contact with our *self*—and yet a rejection of that self, and we are left wondering who and what this self is, at once so intimate and so remote.

These are quite common experiences and may seem trivial. But in fact it is arguable that at the root of them is the attempt to explore and establish one's own identity by anchoring it in time and place and in the sensibly apprehensible. So the questions 'Who am I? What am I?' are not merely the subject of speculation for philosophers, but the concern, no less real for being unconscious, of everyone.

We all argue about dates and times. We all appreciate it when people remember our name. We all locate ourselves by our job, home town and ancestry. What is perhaps new in this century is the violence and articulateness with which this common concern is expressed. Writers today are not merely touching on the subject: they are probing it, continually returning to it, using it often as the basis of all other questions and frequently expressing it emotionally, with fear at the uncertainty about how we can locate ourselves, or anger at what we seem to show ourselves to be. In this generation we have gone further than this. We are not merely asking what we are and how we establish ourselves, but whether we have any identity as a human race at all, whether the question itself is meaningless.

On this, for many of us, all other questions hang. 'On the crude level', runs a recent review of a new play, 'the play makes you wonder not who done it but who are they? On a more cerebral literary level . . . it makes you wonder about political guilt, and typically absurdly, whether anything is worth thinking about at all.'[1]

THE DOUBT BEHIND ALL DOUBT

Modern English literature of the last twelve years or so has been increasingly concerned with this mid-century doubt about man's being and, therefore, with all the questions bound up in it. It is interesting to notice in this connection the continued interest in a book written a century ago, *Alice in Wonderland*, in which Lewis Carroll is exploring the same doubts. If you remember Alice's moderately harrowing adventures in Wonderland you will recall that after undergoing the psychological, not to say material, pressure

[1] *The Guardian*, 12 July 1968; review of a performance of Robert Shaw's *The Man in the Glass Booth*.

of changing environment, companions, activities and physical size, she not unnaturally begins to have doubts about herself. Since all the world seems suddenly to have a different set of responses and significances from those she has learnt to expect, perhaps the change is in her.

She exclaims,

> Dear dear! How queer everything is today! And yesterday things went on just as usual. I wonder if I've been changed in the night? Let me think: *was* I the same when I got up this morning? I almost think I can remember feeling a little different. But if I'm not the same, the next question is, 'Who in the world am I?' Ah, *that's* the great puzzle.

And Alice begins to wonder which of all the children she knows she has turned into.

> I'm sure I'm not Ada, . . . for her hair goes in such long ringlets, and mine doesn't go in ringlets at all; and I'm sure I can't be Mabel, for I know all sorts of things, and she, oh, she knows such a very little! Besides *she's* she, and *I'm* I, and—oh dear, how puzzling it all is! I'll try if I know all the things I used to know. Let me see: four times five is twelve, and four times six is thirteen, and four times seven is—oh dear! I shall never get to twenty at that rate. However, the Multiplication table doesn't signify: let's try Geography. London is the capital of Paris, and Paris is the capital of Rome . . . No, *that's* all wrong, I'm certain. I must have been changed for Mabel! . .[2]

It is valuable to turn back to Alice for two reasons. First, because when she has doubts about the intelligibility of the world and her own place in it, she attempts to establish some basis for certainty by examining her physical appearance (her hair style) and what she herself knows. Her identity as an individual seems to be bound up in some way with what she can sense physically and with the content of her own mind. Second, the idea behind *Alice in Wonderland*, the whole pattern of its development,[3] is that life, viewed with a certain cold, rational clarity, can appear to be a nonsense story,

[2] Lewis Carroll, *Alice's Adventures in Wonderland*, in *The Annotated Alice*, with introduction and notes by Martin Gardner (Penguin, 1965).
[3] See the introduction to *The Annotated Alice*.

Told by an idiot, full of sound and fury,
Signifying nothing.

Both these ideas, the attempt to examine what one indisputably is, and the apparent absurdity of life, are extremely relevant to our understanding of today's climate of opinion and feeling. I say 'feeling' deliberately, because we must be less concerned here with the systematic philosophers than with that complex of feeling and thought, that sense of shared attitudes and beliefs or non-beliefs, which animates any society and which gathers force and bursts out in forms as widely varied as the writings of Iris Murdoch and John Osborne on the one hand, and 'happenings' and 'hippiness' on the other.

THE DRAMATIC QUESTION

Although the forms of expression are varied, there are special reasons why the modern search for identity finds some of its clearest articulation in the writing and acting of plays. One of the reasons is concerned with the nature of drama itself.[4] Arthur Miller analyses it in such a way as to indicate this nature clearly. He assumes always in writing his plays that they will be acted before an audience, and that the actor, therefore, by the mere act of appearing on the stage, poses that audience certain questions. These questions all circle round knowing more of the figure on the stage. Miller's preface to the collected edition summarizes them as 'Who is he? What is he doing here? How does he live, make a living? Who is he related to? Is he rich or poor? What does he think of himself? What do other people think of him and why? What are his hopes and fears and what does he say they are? What does he claim to want and what does he really want?'[5]

Miller's view is that the playwright's task is to select of those questions the significant ones for his material. But the dramatic

[4] *Cf.* Angus Wilson's comment on Samuel Beckett's preoccupation with *man* rather than God: 'This profound concern for man is surely what has increasingly led him away from novels, where he was left with ideas only, to the theatre' (from a review in *The Observer*, 16 July 1967).

[5] Arthur Miller, introduction to *Collected Plays* (Cresset Press, 1958).

situation itself (that is, the fact that an actor and an audience are encountering each other) ensures that those questions will be asked. If the play is sufficiently effective, the audience moves from asking, 'Who is he? What is he?' to either 'Who is man? What is man?', or 'Who am I? What am I?' Often, in modern writing, the play leaves one asking both. For this reason it is valuable, in any very short study of modern literature like this, to concentrate on the way dramatists focus this idea of identity, and part of a later chapter of this book will do just that. This is not to suggest that only dramatists are concerned with the problem, but merely that they often express it most clearly and forcibly. Other kinds of writer explore the same theme, though sometimes less explicitly or more diffusely.

'I'M AFRAID OF US'

For instance, novels as widely different as Kingsley Amis's *Take a Girl Like You* and William Golding's *Lord of the Flies* examine, among other things, the same question.

In *Take a Girl Like You*,[6] Kingsley Amis describes the sequence of events through which the central figure loses her virginity, and he goes on to ask whether she has lost her essential individuality with it. In the last paragraph of the book she reaches, in conversation with her seducer, of whom she is fond and whom she has agreed to marry, a point of halfamused, halfdepressed resignation about her loss of ideals. She wonders whether such a loss in such a world was inevitable:

'You know, Patrick Standish, I should never really have met you. Or I should have got rid of you while I still had the chance. But I couldn't think how to. And it's a bit late for that now, isn't it? I'll just change my dress. Well, those old Bibleclass ideas have certainly taken a knocking, haven't they?'

'They were bound to, you know, darling, with a girl like you. It was inevitable.'

'Oh yes, I expect it was. But I can't help feeling it's rather a pity.'

It's rather a pity. . . Why? In other words, what is the special quality of 'a girl like you' and how is it to be maintained in a

6 Gollancz, 1960.

society like this? Is the pity really to be found in that she has lost her special quality, that which made her an individual, because of the pressure society put on her, that she has been made to conform and thus to lose her identity as a person? Amis's handling of the theme is comic rather than tragic, and he never examines it deeply. He merely suggests in these closing lines that because an individuality has been lost, perhaps something important has been destroyed.

William Golding goes much further. *Lord of the Flies*[7] was published in 1954, and so comes very clearly at that point when writers were beginning to articulate the mid-century sense of the world and man's place in it. Most people will be familiar not only with the outline of the story, but with its theme—the disintegration of individuals and therefore of the society they compose. Golding suggests that the whole future of the race, the whole future indeed of this physical world, depends on safeguarding not only individual personality but the identity of human beings as a race. He sees individual character, the nature of man generally and the significance of the physical universe as all interconnected.

In his story of boys cast away on a desert island, he makes the ordinary objects in their world change their importance as the values of the boys themselves change. A rock, for instance, which was originally something to be admired for its beauty or an object against which one could test one's strength, becomes as the boys' characters deteriorate a murderous weapon, a thing to be used for killing and destruction. The safe ordinariness of everyday objects, therefore, takes on a new dimension of threat or menace in some way connected with what individuals can become, and beneath this what human beings *are*. And so existence in the world *as a human being* becomes inescapably terribly dangerous. 'I'm afraid of *us*', says Ralph, the central character, as the true nature of their predicament becomes clearer to him.

'THE CRYING WENT ON'

Golding shows his boys reflecting the human attempt to build defences against this fear by asserting their individual identity and making doomed attempts to create an ordered and stable society.

[7] Faber and Faber, 1954.

One of the most moving incidents in the book is a minor one which mirrors what the whole novel explores on a larger scale. Early in the book we are introduced to a small boy, survivor of the aircrash on the deserted island, reciting at the request of the other boys the name and address he has been so carefully taught in that other civilized world where he had an identity.

> 'Now tell us. What's your name?'
> 'Percival Wemys Madison, The Vicarage, Harcourt St Anthony, Hants, telephone, telephone, tele—'
> As if this information was rooted far down in the springs of sorrow, the littlun wept. His face puckered, the tears leapt from his eyes, his mouth opened till they could see a square black hole. . . .
> 'Shut up, you! Shut up!'
> Percival Wemys Madison would not shut up. A spring had been tapped, far beyond the reach of authority or even physical intimi-dation. The crying went on, breath after breath, and seemed to sustain him upright as if he were nailed to it.

By the end of the book the menace threatening this community of individuals has been realized, and except for two killed and one hunted for his life all the boys have regressed to savagery with the island in flames about them. When an unexpected ship arrives to rescue them, no detail more clearly indicates their loss of identity as individuals and members of a civilized society than what has happened to this small boy:

> Other boys were appearing now, tiny tots some of them, brown, with the distended bellies of small savages. One of them came close to the officer and looked up.
> 'I'm, I'm—'
> But there was no more to come. Percival Wemys Madison sought in his head for an incantation that had faded clean away.

The sorrow of a small boy in contemplating his lost identity, Golding suggested above, was 'far beyond the reach of authority or even physical intimidation'. His imagery even suggests a sorrow as of the crucifixion. It is at such level of horror and loss that man and his role, who he is and where he stands in the universe, are being scrutinized by writers today. It is at a level where authority and even the desperate violence of the age do not seem adequate, do not seem to reach. To begin to understand this we need to go back a bit, to see what began to shape the movement that is today's writing.

3 DISILLUSIONMENT AND PROTEST
Some preliminary attitudes

It will already have begun to emerge that there are two distinct perspectives in contemporary concern for who and what man is. One focuses on his identity as an individual, that is as a human being uniquely different from all other human beings. The other focuses on his identity as a member of the human race, that is as a creature sharing with all other creatures of the same species a capacity for an existence which has some special meaning. The first is the Kingsley Amis emphasis, exploring what makes a person different from other people, special, unique. The second goes further and really asks if there is anything that makes us corporately unique as human beings—a sort of lowest common denominator. William Golding juxtaposed these two concepts in *Lord of the Flies*. The small boys had not only ceased to be Percival Wemys Madison and Ralph and Jack; there is even the suggestion, brought out particularly clearly in the film of the book, that at moments they had ceased to be recognizable human beings at all.

All this raises a terrifying question. If man as a race is reducible in this way to the non-human, is there any assertable pattern of life at all? Is it possible to argue with integrity, knowing the levels to which humanity can be lowered, that there is a purpose and pattern in existence, that 'good' and 'happiness'—let alone 'God'— are terms with any valid meaning, that anything means anything at all? Is it not truer to man's experience to speak of the 'monstrous mindlessness of the cosmos', to assert, as one writer[1] says *Alice in*

---

[1] Martin Gardner, *op. cit.*

Wonderland does, that 'we all live slapstick lives under an inexplicable sentence of death'?

This is the question which lies behind much serious modern writing. Writers may expound or explore or refute it, but they dare not with integrity ignore it. It is, of course, no new question. The book of Job, for instance, asks it very directly. And before Job finds an answer that satisfies him, he expresses a number of ideas which in their protest and disillusionment come very close to the tone of some of today's writing. For an indication of what modern authors in general are saying, we can turn to *Protest*,[2] a selection of excerpts from current writing on both sides of the Atlantic. In the introduction the editors asked whether the destruction of 'illusion', and the 'acceptance' of life as cruel and horrific, was not the only dignity men could achieve: 'Should man live a slave to illusions he knows to be untrue? Or should he tear down the false front that masks itself as his dignity and thereby enter into an existence wherein, through acceptance of his loneness and of the ever-present possibility of sudden death, he can find the potential for freedom and authentic identity? . . .' Many young people 'accept life as a state of continuing anxiety; they too see man as thirsting for and demanding meaning, even if in the flight from banality they approach the essence of horror'.

This is a complex state of mind. It demolishes most previously held views of our dignity as human beings; dignity now is to be found only in the acceptance of non-dignity, or at least little beyond that of the brute. Yet it asks for 'meaning' in life. The paradoxical nature of this view becomes even clearer when we realize that there is a demand for honesty (which is an ideal) in facing that 'ideals' are meaningless, that they are a fiction of the human race based on an untrue view of the world.

This attitude, obviously generically connected with Sartre and Camus, found its expression in the English-speaking world in the 'beat' writers of America and the 'angry young men' of England. But it was complex because there were present in it both destructive and constructive elements, and these have affected the developing thought of the century in different ways, so that drama and litera-

[2] Eds. G. Feldman and M. Gartenberg (Souvenir Press, 1959; Panther, 1960).

ture have now gone far beyond such labelled and limited move-
ments as 'Beat' and 'Angry'. Nevertheless today's writing took its
beginning from what was felt and written then.

The first impact on writing was the result of the destructive
element in this state of mind. There was, to begin with, a recognition of the fact of violence in human society. Two world wars,
the revealed horrors of Belsen, the planned murder of a nation, the
wave of domestic crime between and after the wars were world
facts which a new generation inherited, and they provided the
perspective in which this generation assessed the meaning of the
creation of the atom and hydrogen bombs. The fact of destructive
power and its probable imminent use conditioned their thinking.
Since a writer expresses the world as he knows it, there was a
developing preoccupation with the delineation of violence, cruelty
and sadism; we shall look at this more closely in connection with
the Theatre of Cruelty.

But many writers, while recognizing these facts, were not content
that violence should be the order of society. They were not ready
to accept that civilization should be demolished by the forces
rampant within it. So they saw their task was to fight destruction.
With Pablo Picasso they understood their art to be 'weapons of
war against brutality and darkness'. Their task meant that on the
one hand they must discover within human society those endur-
ing virtues which were so fundamental to its nature that no
disintegrating powers could shake them.[3] On the other they must
destroy as dangerous all 'pseudo-values', those qualities which
pretended to this virtue but did not really possess it; among such they
classified imperialism, militarism, religious dogmatism and social
convention. They must find the true virtue of being human. They
must destroy whatever had in swollen pretentiousness assumed that
vital integrity without truly possessing it.

[3] Professor Alvarez expounds this very fully in his introduction to
The New Poetry (Penguin, 1962).

It is always easier to knock down than to build up, particularly in
the case of human virtues. So writers generally concentrated on the
second part of their task, the destruction of all those pseudo-values
which seem to have no real virtue in themselves but which can
survive only if we 'do an ostrich' and pretend the dangers to society
are not there. They used all the violence inherent in the age to
attack those clichés to which men have paid lip service, but to
which they felt no real strength or integrity attached; and they did
this at all levels, rating the pseudo-aesthetic, pseudo-intellectual,
pseudo-social, pseudo-religious values of the time as irrelevant, as
not meeting the need of the moment.

D. J. Enright wrote a savage poem called 'Apocalypse'[4] on the
subject of pseudo-values. He bases it on a brief extract from a
German tourist brochure which tells how, by the early summer of
1945, 'while the town still reeked of smoke, charred buildings and
the stench of corpses, the Philharmonic Orchestra bestowed the
everlasting and imperishable joy which music never fails to give'.
And after the 'Newer Apocalypse' (the atomic war), will we
find the same . . .?

> It soothes the savage doubts.
> One Bach outweighs ten Belsens . . .
>
> After the Newer Apocalypse, very few members
> Were still in possession of their instruments
> (Very few were still in possession of their members),
> And their suits were chiefly indecent.
> Yet while the town still reeked of smoke etc.,
> The Philharmonic trio bestowed etc.
>
> A civilisation vindicated,
> A race with three legs to stand on!
> True, the violin was later silenced by leukaemia

[4] In *Addictions* (Chatto and Windus, 1962).

And the pianoforte crumbled softly into dust.
But the flute was left. And one is enough.
All, in a sense, goes on. All is in order.

And the ten-tongued mammoth larks,
And the forty-foot crickets and the elephantine frogs
Decided that the little chap was harmless,
At least he made no noise, on the banks of whatever river it used
to be.

One day, a reed warbler stepped on him by accident.
However, all, in a sense, goes on. Still the everlasting and
imperishable joy
Which music never fails to give is being given.

The fury informing this poem is caused by men's refusal to face
reality, a kind of 'fiddling while Rome burns', escaping into an
illusory world of aesthetic beauty which is false because it has
divorced itself completely from the current situation, instead of
saying something relevant to it. It is this same fury which we find
behind much of the vigour of writing in the mid-fifties.

John Wain, for example, wrote a vigorous but comic analysis
of society in his novel *Hurry on Down*[5] and John Osborne a
vigorously angry one in the play *Look Back in Anger*.[6] The dominant
mood, in other words, is one of protest, and whether the result is
comic or serious the motive is *attack*, on civilized virtues which
pretend to be adequate and are not:

> . . . loudly for Truth have liars pled,
> their heels for Freedom slaves will click;
> where Boobs are holy, poets mad
> illustrious punks of Progress shriek.[7]

These 'false' values are examined in many different contexts.
The two writers just mentioned, John Wain and John Osborne,

[5] Secker and Warburg, 1953.
[6] Faber and Faber, 1956.
[7] From E. E. Cummings, 'Jehovah buried, Satan dead', *Selected Poems 1923–58* (Faber and Faber, 1960).

are among those who concern themselves principally with social values. They attack the materialism and complacency which, disguised under the names of 'affluence' and 'respectability', are the chief values of suburbia.

Giles Cooper takes this much further than either of them, in his play *Everything in the Garden*,[8] a horror comedy in which he suggests that to safeguard affluence and respectability the suburban wives will prostitute themselves and the suburban husbands will lie and kill.

This materialism and complacency on a national level is seen to be located in an 'Establishment' of government, education, army and church. Arnold Wesker, John Braine, John Arden, William Golding, Muriel Spark, Max Frisch, Shelagh Delaney, Peter Shaffer and many others have all been concerned during the last twelve years with different effects of such social pseudo-values.

'DO-GOODING': GOVERNMENT AND THE WELFARE STATE

Perhaps one of the clearest examples of this is in Adrian Mitchell's contemporary ballad, 'Fifteen Million Plastic Bags'.[9] The plastic bag represents at once the symbol of material progress and the facelessness and ultimate death of those who put the plastic bags over their heads, over their brains, so that they do not think any more, do not call into question what society tells them. It is the Establishment—the government (to whom the warehouse belongs) and the priest—who are involved in this 'murder by plastic bag'.

> I was walking in a government warehouse
> Where the daylight never goes
> I saw fifteen million plastic bags
> Hanging in a thousand rows.
>> And five million bags were six feet long
>> Five million were five feet five
>> Five million were stamped with Mickey Mouse
>> And they came in a smaller size.

8 Penguin, 1968.
9 In *Poems* (Jonathan Cape, 1964).

34

Were they for guns or uniforms
Or a dirty kind of party game?
Then I saw each bag had a number
And every bag bore a name.
   And five million bags were six feet long, *etc.*

So I've taken my bag from its hanger
And I've pulled it over my head
And I'll wait for the priest to zip it
So the radiation won't spread.
   And five million bags are six feet long, *etc.*

There is, however, a more subtle social value than respectability and affluence which some protest writers are quick to note. This is something endemic in any Welfare State: the 'do-gooding' attitude of mind sometimes found in, for instance, the welfare worker who does not see those on the receiving end of his good works as living, breathing, human beings with their own claim to dignity, however fallen.

The best-known writing on this topic is probably Alan Sillitoe's *The Loneliness of the Long-distance Runner.*[1] The runner is a Borstal boy, who is being encouraged by the Governor of his institution to win the race between the local public school and the Borstal. But the boy suspects that it is not for his own sake, but for the honour and glory, perhaps of the institution, certainly of the Governor, who thinks no more of the boy than he would of a race horse he had never seen but on which he had placed a bet. And so the boy says bitterly,

> And I'll lose that race, because I'm not a race horse at all, and I'll let him know it when I'm about to get out . . . I'm a human being and I've got thoughts and secrets and bloody life inside me that he doesn't know is there, and he'll never know what's there because he's stupid.

So a potential social good is falsified, becomes a pseudo-value, because it is incompetently effected by someone so ham-handed and

[1] W. H. Allen, 1960.

unaware that he denies by his attitude the worth of the human being he is trying to help.

In John Hopkins's television quartet of plays, *Talking to a Stranger*,[2] which we shall be looking at more closely later, we see one of the most recently developed expositions of this, and its effect on the recipient. Terry is expecting an illegitimate baby. Her independent spirit failing her, she turns to her married brother, Alan, for help; but she arrives in the middle of the night and so threatens his domestic peace. His wife, Ellen, is not likely to be sympathetic.

> TERRY: I won't stay. Thanks all the same.
> ALAN: What?
> TERRY: It's too much trouble.
> ALAN: No trouble at all. Ellen knows. . . .
> TERRY: (harshly) What—does Ellen know. . . ? I'm potty—sort of demented child liable to turn up in the middle of the night—any night—and ask—what?—for sanctuary?
> ALAN: No.
> TERRY: I'd rather go—oh, you know—somewhere I have to pay. Somewhere I have—rights.
> ALAN: For goodness sake, Terry—the nearest hotel. . . .
> TERRY: People you pay don't—say no. . . . I'll ring a doorbell. Pay up—look happy—and go to sleep.

It is a fair protest. Any charity, any work of good, which loses sight of the worth of the recipient in the glorious worth of the deed is of questionable value. That is what these writers are stating. And we may ourselves be guilty of perpetuating these pseudo-values in society. As the wave of goodwill towards well-doing, whether conceived in Christian or humanistic terms, gathers momentum, it becomes increasingly necessary to examine one's own motives. Why do I join VSO, or serve with Christian Aid? To enlarge my own experience? To enjoy the pleasure of 'doing good' to people?

The writers we have mentioned are in fact emphasizing the need for maintaining and upholding the worth of the individual

[2] Penguin, 1967.

36

in the same way that the Christian faith does. The Christ of the Gospels (who for the humanist as well as the Christian remains the archetype of self-giving) never made the recipients of His help feel belittled by it. On the contrary, by respecting them as individuals He was able to transform their lives, to enable them to realize their own potential worth, to recognize their identity as people created by God, in His image.

Behind the lack of awareness and sensitivity that Hopkins and Sillitoe—and many others—describe, there is sometimes something deeper and more dangerous. There is the moral self-seeking which is very closely akin to spiritual pride, a 'holier than thou' attitude in *social* terms. Kingsley Amis has a group of short stories collected under the title *My Enemy's Enemy*[3] which expresses this very clearly. One of these stories, called 'Moral Fibre', makes the central figure speak of a social worker with whom he is involved in a case:

> The woman's a menace, a threat to Western values. Terrifying to think of her being a social worker. All that awful knowing-best stuff, being quite sure what's good for people and not standing any nonsense and making them knuckle under and going round saying how fully she appreciates the seriousness and importance of her job, as if that made it all right. . . .
>
> Meanwhile I put to myself the question whether the removal of all social workers, preferably by execution squads, wouldn't do everyone a power of good. You had to do something about ill-treated etc. children all right, but you could see to that without behaving like a sort of revivalist military policeman. . . .
>
> In any contact not made on terms of equality the speech of one party or the other will fall almost inevitably into the accents and idioms of patronage.

So even those attempts society has made to counter its own disintegration by ambulance work among its misfits are seen as of questionable value because they are too superficial, not concerned at a deep enough level.

[3] Gollancz, 1962.

Social welfare work, however, is not the only vaunted remedy which is seen as inadequate and even false by the protest writers. Education has been another much-heralded cure for society's ills; but writers of the mid-century were as violent in their attack on false intellectual values as they were on false social ones. Pseudo-culture takes as vigorous a beating as any, because again its positive value can be subordinated to the social advancement or material welfare of its participants. Hence the popularity of *Lucky Jim*,[4] Kingsley Amis's novel which guyed the young lecturer, representative of the new wave of mass education, shouldering others out of his way as they shouldered him, all concerned to knock up a living out of academics, but none of them genuinely concerned about intellectual values.

His poetic equivalent can be found in Brian Higgins's 'The North'[5] in which he uses Hull and its university as a convenient target for an attack which is really aimed at the more general failure of education because of its pseudo-values.

> The stark rectangle of Hull
> With its bombed squares filling up even now
> Twenty years after the Luftwaffe gave it a going over
> Stands by the wide desolation of the Humber.
> A cold clean city full of new pubs
> With the worst university in England
> Peopled with foreman-lecturers jostling to get reviews in the
>   *Guardian*
> Even their names sound like pieces of machinery.
>
> The 'English Department' runs a Critical Quarterly
> A kind of correspondence seminar for schoolgirls
> That's about as well written as a TV advert.
> A few prim little verses by the interior decorators of the '50s
> And critical articles that read like bills of lading.
> The library card index is presided over by a sad poet
> A beat-up Beverley Nichols all kodaks and missed chances

---

[4] Gollancz, 1954.
[5] In *The Only Need* (Abelard-Schuman, 1961).

Out to catch 'the Great Pleasure-Loving Public'
What with? a butterfly net?

The new proletarian intellectuals
Who have beer and darts parties ('My father was a crane driver')
All the uniform muddle of the New Left
Competing like hell to get their articles published.
And Lucky-Jimming it up to Senior Lecturer.
Pretending to boast about having a refrigerator
But really winking at knowing what refrigerators stand for.
Interviewing the surrounding chaos and insurance stamping us to
    Elysium
Till the cellars burst and the statistics rattle the ceiling
(I'd rather jump into a tankful of Chablis and to hell with the
    social survey
And social justice into the bargain, if that's what they call it)
DON'T BLAME ME, I'M NOT ADAM.

Brian Higgins is bitter with disillusionment at the aridity and gracelessness of life in this 'uniform muddle' which does not give what 'education' promised (hence the yearning for a tankful of Chablis). It is not adequate, does not begin to be adequate, to satisfy, to meet the powerful impact of that violence and sadism spoken of earlier.[6]

THE ARMY

How to contend, then, with society in eruption? By a well-drilled army to put down any trouble as it arises? Is the virtue of a human society its capacity to mobilize itself to put down by physical violence whatever threatens the *status quo*? The Armed Forces have a high tradition of service and discipline. Yet they, too, are under fire.

Arnold Wesker, John Arden and John Whiting all attack the virtues of military discipline and *esprit de corps* as others had

[6] Other writers who attack pseudo-intellectualism include Angus Wilson, *The Mulberry Bush* (Secker and Warburg, 1956); Peter Shaffer, *Five Finger Exercise* (Hamish Hamilton, 1958); Robert Bolt, *The Tiger and the Horse* (Heinemann, 1961).

attacked moral welfare and education. *Chips with Everything*,[7] *Sergeant Musgrave's Dance*[8] and *Marching Song*,[9] although totally different dramatically, all contain savage indictments of the necessary suppression of human fellowship and mutual respect in order to achieve the perfected military machine, the 'disciplined corps' which can 'put down' society's insurrections.

In *Chips with Everything* this is shown at two levels: first, the horrific bayonet practice in which men are reduced to charging animals in the necessity to kill others rather than themselves be killed:

> *The square. A dummy is hanging. It is bayonet practice for the squad.*
> HILL: Even officers must go through this. Everyone, but everyone must know how to stick a man with a bayonet. The occasion may not arise to use the scorching thing but no man passes through this outfit till he's had practice. It's a horrible thing, this. A nasty weapon and a nasty way to kill a man. But it is you or him. A nasty choice, but you must choose. . . . So! Again, hold the butt and drop the muzzle—so. Lean forward, crouch, and let me see the horriblest leer your face can make. Then, when I call 'attack' I want to see you rush towards that old straw dummy, pause, lunge and twist your knife with all the hate you can. And one last thing—the scream. I want to hear you shout your lungs out, cos it helps. A horde of screaming men put terror in the enemy and courage in themselves. It helps. Get fell in, two ranks. Front rank will assume the on-guard position—ON GUARD! Run, scream, lunge!
>
> *(Hill demonstrates it himself. One by one the men rush forward at the dummy, until it comes to Pip. He stands still.)*
> I said attack. Thompson, you, that's you. Are you gone daft? I've given you an order—run, scream, you. Are you refusing to obey? A/C2 Thompson I have ordered you to use your bayonet . . .
>
> A/C2 Thompson, I am about to issue you with a legitimate order according to Her Majesty's rules and regulations, Section Ten paragraph five, and I must warn you that failing to carry out this order will result in you being charged under Section Ten paragraph sixteen of the same book . . . I am now about to give the command. Wait for it and think carefully—this is only practice and no one

[7] Jonathan Cape, 1962. [8] Grove Press, 1962. [9] Heinemann, 1955.

can be hurt. Within ten seconds it will all be over, that's advice. Attack.

(Silence. No movement.)

Squad—slope ARMS! A/C2 Thompson—I'm charging you with failure to obey a legitimate order issued by an NCO in command under Her Majesty's Air Force, and may God help you, lad.

But at a deeper level the military pattern is shown as corrupting the ideals of the individual who attempts to stand out against it, demolishing them, taking and twisting them. Pip, who refuses bayonet practice, has also refused to accept a commission because it would mean, he feels, accepting the whole military ethos and denying his relationship with his fellows, the other ranks. His offensive is crushed by the Pilot Officer in charge: 'We listen but do not hear, we befriend but do not touch you, we applaud but we do not act—to tolerate is to ignore.'

And when Pip is brought on a charge for refusing the bayonet practice with all it implies to him of dehumanization, the two ideas are brought together. The Pilot Officer refuses him a court martial and strips down the motives for his behaviour, suggesting that beneath the 'comradeship'—'the affinity of one human being to another'—beneath the 'guilt' because of his fellow-beings' suffering, beneath, perhaps, though doubtfully, 'modesty', there lies the desire for power. Pip is making gestures, he hints, in order to win 'among the good-natured yobs' respect he secretly desires and cannot gain among his own kind. Since this accusation has just been made by those same 'good-natured yobs', this is too much for Pip, and he breaks down:

PIP: Oh God—

PILOT OFFICER: God? God? Why do you call upon God? Are you his son? Better still, then. You are found out even more, illusions of grandeur, Thompson. We know that also, that's what we know, that's what we have, the picture you have of yourself, and now that we know that, you're really finished, destroyed. You're destroyed, Thompson. . . .

And Thompson *is* destroyed. With a deliberate use of Christian imagery Wesker makes this man who had faintly glimpsed his identity as a son of God act the part of Peter's denial. He goes back to the bayonet ground, undergoes the dehumanizing, and with three screams and three lunges denies three times his proper human identity.

This protest is still an issue. The ideals of service and patriotism, even if they are recognized as potentially good, are still bitterly questioned: are they a danger because in their very goodness they blind men to the greater good which is being destroyed by them? When our troops are sent to keep order in some remote part of the world, what is the cost in physical, moral, spiritual terms? Is it too high? Is it being wrongfully paid?

For seven years at school I named
   Our kings, their wars—if these were won—
A boy trained simple as we come,
   I read of an island in the sun,
   Where the Queen of Love was born.

At seventeen the postman brought
   Into the room—my place of birth—
Some correspondence from the Crown,
   Demanding that with guns I earn
   The modern shilling I was worth.

Lucky for me that I could read,
   Lucky for me our captain said,
You'll see the world for free, my son,
   You're posted to an island, John,
   Where the Queen of Love was born. . . .

When morning came our captain bold
   Said the island shaped like an ass's skin
Must be kept calm, must be patrolled,
   For outposts are the heart and soul
   Of empire, love, and lawful rule.

I did not know to serve meant kill,
   And I did not see the captain fall,

As my life went out through a bullet hole,
  Mother, I said, your womb is done,
  Did they spend your English shilling well ?[1]

THE CHURCH

The 'Establishment', we suggested earlier, was represented in the minds of many writers of the fifties by government, education, army and church. And we have to recognize that much of the attack by 'protest' writers on the church was justified. They found in some aspects of ecclesiastical hierarchy and ritual the same adherence to dead formulae, the same complacency, the same total lack of awareness of people and their needs, that had been spotlighted in other parts of the Establishment. There was often a lack of vitality, a lack of urgency of belief, beautifully caught by Paul Dehn in 'A Modern Hymnal':[2]

  Onward, Christian soldiers,
  Each to war resigned,
  With the Cross of Jesus
  Vaguely kept in mind.

Because of this it was felt that the church had nothing to say to the people's need, people as they *are* in today's society. John Osborne expresses this most movingly in *The Entertainer*:[3]

  Have you ever got on a railway train here, got on a train from Birmingham to West Hartlepool? Or gone from Manchester to Warrington or Widnes. And you get out, you go down the street, and on one side maybe is a chemical works and on the other side is the railway goods yard. Some kids are playing in the street and you walk up to some woman standing on her doorstep. It isn't a doorstep really because you can walk straight from the street into her front room. What can you say to her? What real piece of in-

[1] From Christopher Logue, 'Song of the Dead Soldier', *Songs* (Hutchinson, 1959).

[2] In *The Fern on the Rock, Collected Poems 1935–65* (Hamish Hamilton, 1965).

[3] Faber and Faber, 1961; first performed in 1957.

formation, what message can you give to her? Do you say: 'Madam, d'you know that Jesus died on the Cross for you?' . . . And then the woman, she looks back at you, and she says, 'O yes, I heard all about that.'

E. L. Mascall put into verse what had happened for many, to whom the church had become synonymous with culture and wealth, not with the burning faith that transformed men's lives and made them ready and happy to die for their Lord:

Tell me not, Dean, I am unkind
  If from the snuggery
Of thy well-furnished, cultured mind
  To Chelsea's strand I fly.

Where England's Chancellor by grace
  Of holiness was steeled
To meet the tyrant face to face,
  To die and not to yield.

And though, of course, his views were such
  As you will still deplore,
I could not love thee Dean, so much,
  Loved I not Thomas More.[4]

The result of this in many people's attitude was epitomized by such plays as *The Making of Moo* by Nigel Dennis, or *Miss Pulkinhorn* by William Golding. In *The Making of Moo*,[5] Nigel Dennis builds up dramatically a pseudo-religion in order to suggest that the Christian faith as it is practised in the mid-twentieth century pretends to a virtue it does not possess, preaches a dogma which is not relevant to its practice, and therefore has nothing to say to a society in convulsions. (Dennis would go further and say that it is based on a myth which needs exploding.) *Miss Pulkinhorn*[6] is a radio play based on an incident in a cathedral where a devout adherent, an elderly lady, her devotions disturbed by the undisciplined adoration of a simple-minded regular worshipper,

[4] 'To a dignitary who spoke contemptuously of a saint', *Pi in the High* (Faith Press, 1959).

[5] In *Two Plays and a Preface* (Weidenfeld and Nicolson, 1958).

[6] First broadcast in 1960.

takes steps to prevent this, breaks his heart, and is in a real sense his murderess. I mention these two totally different plays together because the gist of their attack is the same: the unreality of the faith preached by the church in general *through its practice*. Thus it comes under attack for its pseudo-value.

All these 'protest' writers begin by saying what is in fact an implication of Christian belief, that no declaration of values, no social administration or improvement, however praiseworthy for its good intention, is of any real effect or relevance if it does not take into account the nature of society and the nature of man. This is where the protest writers speak truth, and this is why they should be heard.

They insist that all attempts to meet the needs of man must be based on the reality of man as he is, and a respect for him as he is, not as we should like him to be when we have finished with him. In their stripping away of the pretentious and the unrealistic, the morally and spiritually inflated, they have spoken justly and rightly, and however much one may disagree with some of their premises, one can only be grateful for the truth they have insisted on, and the falsehoods they have destroyed.

But of course there is a great gap between the Christian understanding of society and that of Osborne or Wesker or the majority of writers I have mentioned. The Christian sees society as rooted in the bond between God and man, finding there its final perspective and values. Society is in one sense 'man in relationship'; and for the Christian all relationships, whether group or individual, can be determined only by that existing between man and his Creator. The pattern of society, its rules and administration, what it does about its misfits and how well it does it, are the fruit of this much deeper evaluation of what life is about and what man is. A non-Christian writer—one, in fact, violently anti-Christian—was clear enough on this:

> For several reasons morals cannot be slapped on superficially as a social lubricant. They must share a common basis with social organisation and be consistent with accepted knowledge. You cannot, that is, 'have the fruit without the root'.[7]

[7] Edward Bond, preface to *Saved* (Methuen, 1966).

45

This is where Christians must be quite explicit. The protest writers' attack on the falseness of so much in the social fabric is justified but Christians would say that there always *will* be a falseness as long as society tries to create its own justice out of its own body, without reference to the God behind and in society. David Gascoyne puts this splendidly:

> There is no perfectly just man
> Because the vision of Justice is the pleasure of God alone.
> And that is why the divine part in all men
> Longs to see justice and to live by it;
> While the enemy of God that is in each of us
> Is always trying to make us satisfied with what we can see of
>   Justice without God,
> As though He were bound to ratify automatically
> Whatever man-made judge with his own reason decides is just
> Provided a sufficiently large number of other men be persuaded
>   to agree with him.[8]

'Right' and 'justice', therefore, in the Christian view, are the monopoly of God alone, whether applied in society or in individual life; and we learn more of them as we learn more of Him in the terms of our everyday living. God is not good because He approves of justice; it is the other way round. Justice is good because it is God's will.

[8] From 'Fragments towards a *religio poetae*', *Collected Poems* (OUP, 1965). David Gascoyne, born in 1916, was writing in the late thirties, but remains an importantly relevant writer at this late stage of the century. His *Collected Poems* was a Poetry Book Society recommendation in 1965.

4 'MY OWN AND THE HUMAN SPIRIT'
A causal relationship

WHERE RESPONSIBILITY LIES

It was inevitable that once society had been searchingly examined for the values which should be effective in it and for the dangers under which it stood, a shift of focus would follow in which a scrutiny was made of the individual's relationship to all this. How far was the private world of the individual in any way connected with the visible disintegration of society? The threat to civilization of total violence shattering all forms and patterns of group life arises from that very civilization, from its national organization of violence to certain permitted ends. In the same way, the threat to individuals is seen today as emerging from the very nature of those individuals themselves.

Professor Alvarez in his introduction to *The New Verse* points out how modern authors are aware of the same forces at work within individual human beings as can be seen at work in society, and links this with Bruno Bettelheim's psycho-analytical work in Dachau and Buchenwald. Bettelheim records how he recognized in the actions of the guards in those concentration camps his own desires of cruelty and hate. There is a sense of guilt in modern writing, because we see around us that which echoes ourselves.

Iris Murdoch is perhaps the best-known novelist to analyse, with great delicacy, such a theme. In *The Unicorn*[1] she builds up a fantasy world in which all the characters are mesmerized by the problematical guilt or innocence of the central figure round whom

[1] Chatto and Windus, 1963.

they revolve. *The Bell*[2] is even more specific in relating individual responsibility and collective guilt.

There is a quality of fantasy, or rather nightmare (as Valerie Pitt has pointed out[3]) about another writer relevant here. Richard Hughes created, in *The Fox in the Attic*,[4] a study of the changing Germany during the rise of Adolf Hitler. This book is particularly appropriate here, because the individual who mirrors the destruction of a society in his own inner life is the central figure who shaped German national history in the twenties and thirties: Adolf Hitler himself. Richard Hughes suggests that for Hitler life was centred upon himself, and there were no other *persons* in the universe, only *things*. The point of this for us here is, first, that Hitler, envisaged in such terms, is an excellent example of the individual, like society, failing to recognize the nature and worth of human beings and paying the penalty of his blindness and false vision. Second, this failure of understanding on the part of one individual —albeit a powerful one politically—is seen in direct causal relationship to the collapse of that society.

Doris Lessing takes this a stage further. In 'The Eye of God in Paradise', a story published in a collection called *The Habit of Loving*,[5] she examines the complex sense in which the individual, the ordinary member of the public, is both the moral product of his race and at the same time the agent by whom the moral shape of that race is determined. Each of the main figures in the story represents, by his or her individual conflicts and surrenders, aspects of the moral suicide of a nation. Dr Schröder, for instance, whose face is hideously patched up after burns from a tank explosion, entertains his British guests with obsequiousness because he wants their help, and with angry contempt for what they have done to his nation. His guests are helpless to aid him:

> They were, at this moment, feeling something of the despair that people like them had felt ten, fifteen years ago, watching the tides of madness rise while the reasonable and the decent averted their eyes.

[2] Chatto and Windus, 1958.
[3] *The Writer and the Modern World*, pp. 66–68.
[4] Chatto and Windus, 1961.
[5] MacGibbon and Kee, 1957.

At the same time they were feeling an extraordinary but undeniable reluctance to face the fact that Dr Schröder might represent any more than himself. . . .

But after a humiliating evening's entertainment in which the entire audience join in a pointed satire which expresses, with elaborate courtesy, the depths of furious revengeful humiliation of the nation, they begin to recognize that this individual is also in a deep sense Germany, that he summed it up and presented it to them direct and unambiguously, in such a way that they must reject or accept it. And this leads them to the inevitable next step: 'One nation is not very different from another.' What therefore in Britain corresponds to Dr Schröder?

> What unpleasant forces are this moment simmering in the sewers of our national soul that might explode suddenly? . . . And what deplorable depths of complacency must there be in us . . . that we should feel so superior to Dr Schröder? . . .

And so with each figure in the story; the girl Lili, for example, who says to every conquering American soldier who passes, 'Yank-ee, Yank-ee . . . I love you, buddy', just as her mother

> was in love with our Führer, yes it is true. And before that in love with a Communist leader who lived in our street. And now I tell my Lili it is lucky that she falls in love with the American army, because she is in love with democracy;

the tragic figure of Dr Kroll who runs a mental hospital and spends six months of every year in it as a voluntary patient, whose release is in painting pictures which reflect the two halves of his life, and who speaks of the virtues of the Nazi system of 'social hygiene' which exterminated the physically undesirable; and finally the pathetic figure of the five-year-old boy in the mental hospital 'who bites if you go too near him' and who, 'naked save for a strait-jacket, tied to bars like an animal, was grinding his teeth and glaring at the fat knitting wardress'. All these are seen as expressing in their individual lives the anger and violence, fear and despair, heedlessness and irresponsibility, which had torn their nation apart. But they are not merely national in their implication. They are human.

It is this sense of the relationship between the individual and humanity *in general*, all sense of racialism left behind, which is worked out most movingly and explicitly by Laurens van der Post in *Venture to the Interior*[6] and *The Seed and the Sower*.[7] In the first he speaks of the need to come to terms with the 'black brother within us', examining at that point the problem of race relations and seeing it in terms of our own divided selves. In *The Seed and the Sower* he takes this even further. He traces the history of an officer who met a terrible death in a Japanese prisoner-of-war camp, showing how that officer saw the war in which he was involved as an extension of the treason in his own spirit which had destroyed trust between his brother and himself. He first, on leave, makes reparation privately to his brother, and then, in the prisoner-of-war camp, surrenders himself to a martyr's death in order to avert the guard's anger from his fellow-soldiers. And this he sees as the inevitable movement of a life now committed to healing the breaches for which the guilt of his own spirit had been responsible in his private life and in the world's.

'I am concerned only', he says, 'with the betrayal, with the seed of negation within me, with a particular botany of my own and the human spirit.' He speaks of the first realization 'that the war I was fighting was in me long before it was in the world without. I realized that I was fighting it in a . . . secondary dimension of reality.' He could not suddenly contract out of a situation which he had helped to bring about; for, he felt, we were all 'accessories to the fact of war'.

Van der Post is speaking not only for the philosophers or the intellectually aware: he is speaking for a whole generation whose protest songs include 'The Universal Soldier':[8]

> He's five feet two and he's six feet four,
> He fights with missiles and with spears:
> He's all of thirty-one and he's only seventeen,
> He's been a soldier for a thousand years. . . .

---

[6] Chatto and Windus, 1960.   [7] Hogarth Press, 1963.
[8] Words by Buffy Sainte-Marie.

And he's fighting for Canada
  He's fighting for France
  He's fighting for the USA
And he's fighting for the Russians
  He's fighting for Japan
And he thinks he'll put an end to war this way. . . .

He's the one who gives his body as a weapon to the war,
And without him all the killing can't go on;
He's the Universal Soldier and he really is to blame,
His orders come from far away no more.
They come from here and there and you and me. . . .

Such a song removes the responsibility from the statesman solely
and places it squarely on those who carry out the orders. It lacks,
of course, the perception van der Post shows in extending this
responsibility to every human being who in some way, if only in
thought, is at variance with his neighbour, his family, his brother.
Once such a view of individual human responsibility is accepted,
the traditional negative response of 'hating the guts' of any oppo-
sition/enemy is called into question. Its basis is examined and the
instinctive divisions between human beings are no longer seen as a
justification for conflict. There has to be something more, a belief,
a cause; this idea must be examined in more detail in the next
chapter.

It would be useful to pause and look back to see how we reached
this point. Society, writers are saying, is disintegrating because it
pays lip-service to conventions and ideals but has no genuine
values to withstand the violence it has created for itself. The only
value widely accepted by such writers as valid is the worth of being
human. But when this is looked at more closely, the same dy-
namics of hypocrisy and violence are found in the individual
human; he is responsible in his individual life, therefore, for what
is happening on a larger scale in society. Even his private world is
effective in influencing the movement of nations; Louis MacNeice
writes of London after the last war:

And nobody rose, only some meaningless
Buildings and the people once more were strangers

At home with no one, sibling or friend.
Which is why now the petals fall
Fast from the flower of cities all.[9]

There is nothing new in all this: 'I am involved in the human race' said John Donne in the seventeenth century. 'Ask not for whom the bell tolls; it tolls for thee.' But the *extent* of this realization is new, and, more important still, the sense of urgency and immediacy about it. It is an urgent truth because now, by a clearly seen link of cause and effect, my own hypocrisy is envisaged as directly related to world disintegration.

It is interesting to note that writers are groping their way through to an understanding of evil inherent in the heart of man which is akin to the Christian view of man. 'For the heart is deceitful above all things and desperately corrupt', recorded Jeremiah in the Old Testament. The children wept for 'the end of innocence and the darkness of man's heart', wrote William Golding. But the Christian understanding of the nature of that darkness differs from the popular modern view, as does the Christian hope. For the Old Testament writers asserted that there is light for man, if only he acknowledges and trusts completely the God who has revealed Himself to man, if he recognizes that his darkness comes from his failure to serve the God of love who created him. And so society was repeatedly urged to return to obedience to its Lord wherein lay its health. Individual men were challenged to recognize that their personal darkness might be dissipated did they acknowledge themselves to be God's created beings.

Modern writers hold out no such hope (except for a few, such as Norman Nicholson, Christopher Fry, Patric Dickinson, R. S. Thomas and T. S. Eliot). Yet two positive responses have emerged from this present-day awareness that human beings have the seed of society's disintegration within themselves, and these responses lead us to the deepest inquiry of all that literature is making. The first we look at now: the second we must examine more closely in a later chapter.

[9] From 'Goodbye to London', reprinted in *Poems 1967* (Critical Quarterly Poetry Supplement No. 8).

The first positive response was the desire to portray man as he really is, not as we should like him to be. So entered into literature the figure of the anti-hero, the central character no longer idealized but described with, if anything, his weaknesses and vices to the fore. This was Jimmy Porter in *Look Back in Anger*, Robert Lamb and Ned Roper in *The Contenders*, Beattie in *Roots* and even, though in a different sense, Lord Claverton in *The Elder Statesman*.[1] Nor were his surroundings idealized. This is what man is like and this is the kind of world the majority of us live in, writers were saying. Respect him, feel for him, sorrow for him because he is human, not for virtues he does not possess and the camouflage of comforts which hide what life is really like.

But the cult of the anti-hero was to become deeper in its importance, and the seeds of this development also can be seen in Jimmy Porter's behaviour in *Look Back in Anger*.[2] When he viciously lashes out against his wife, when in despair and longing he tries to beat her emotionally into some kind of response, he is the prototype of all those figures who are used by writers as a kind of therapy, an 'acting out' of the emotions of cruelty, hatred, despair and remorse which are part of the inner knowledge of every human being. Literature here is being used quite deliberately as a kind of safety valve, a form of catharsis whereby authors and readers can, by feeling 'with' the central figure, express their own violence and possibly purge themselves of it.

THE THEATRE OF CRUELTY

This is one of the major elements of the Theatre of Cruelty, the factor which Edward Bond, David Rudkin and Edward Albee, for example, are using. Some of the poets of the 'Group' do the same thing; George Macbeth's verse has some good examples of it. It is given, in some cases, an almost ritualistic setting in order to satisfy the 'need' of the participators, and the link here with the religious orgy of the ancient cults, for example the Dionysian, is worth noting. For in both we find an inexorable movement of

[1] See further, pp. 85 ff.   [2] See further, p. 67.

ritualistic pattern to a climax in which the appetite for violence and sexual excitement finds satiety within a framework to which all participants have given (perhaps reluctant) consent. David Rudkin's play *Afore Night Come*,[3] for instance, includes the ritual killing at harvest time of the stranger who comes to pick fruit.

Now we must be very clear about the issues raised here. It seems to me that, while a case can be made for the Theatre of Cruelty and its parallels in poetry and prose, there are three strong objections to this kind of writing. The first has been well expressed by G. S. Fraser, who saw in such concentration on the cruel and the violent the dangers of a narrowing and perverted vision of life as a whole. In *The Modern Writer and His World*[4] he writes:

> I think also that the more we allow ourselves to go on brooding with a lingering perverse pleasure on the nasty things that can happen in the world, the more likely they are to happen. If all contemporary (writing) were, in vivid detail, about cruelty and madness, I would not take that as a happy sign. There are many hellish things that have happened in the world about which the best advice is still Dante's: 'Take one look and move onwards.' I hope that the race will move onwards . . .

So there is the danger of becoming so wholly involved in violence that we can see nothing else in life. And there is, as Donald Davie is quoted as saying, 'something other than pain'.

The second is akin to this. It is that too much deliberate self-immersion in the cruelty and horror of which one is aware in life (and of which one must *not* be heedless), can lead to a blunting of sensitivity, to the very thing writers are trying to make their public avoid. There is a good example of this in Edward Bond's *Saved*.[5] He attempts to shock his audience into awareness of daily cruelty in the fabric of their lives by staging the killing of a baby on the stage. But his own comments in his preface to the play indicate the danger of this. Speaking of this incident he says:

> Clearly the stoning to death of a baby in a London park is a typical English understatement. Compared to the 'strategic' bombing of

[3] Penguin, 1963.   [4] André Deutsch and Penguin, 1964.
[5] Methuen, 1966; first performed in 1965.

German towns it is a negligible atrocity, compared to the cultural and emotional deprivation of most of our children its consequences are insignificant.

Mr Bond is being deliberately provocative here, and I would not take issue with him on the horror he feels at the bombing of cities and the deprivation of our children: but his use of comparative standards suggests a blunting of that very moral sense about which he is concerned. The death of a baby by stoning is as absolute in its horror as the death of a million people in gas chambers: there is no such thing as a 'negligible atrocity': and the 'consequences' of any act of cruelty can never, *on any terms*, be called 'insignificant'. Such value attaches to human life, however brief or remote from importance in worldly terms, that anything which offends against it is of enormous significance morally. This is not merely good humanism. It is also a fundamental Chrisitan belief. 'Are not five sparrows sold for two pennies? And not one of them is forgotten before God. Why, even the hairs of your head are all numbered. Fear not; you are of more value than many sparrows.'[6]

But there is an even deeper objection to the work of some writers today, and we can perhaps best approach it through comparison with some terrible and yet great play of the past. Is there any distinction to be made between the effect of the Theatre of Cruelty upon an audience emotionally, morally and spiritually, and the effect of, for instance, a play like *King Lear* with its putting out of eyes, its storm scenes of raving madness and the pathos of the unhinged mind, its murder by hanging of the pure and innocent Cordelia, its death by poison of one of the villains and its slow ending in grief at the old king's death?

> The weight of this sad time we must obey;
> Speak what we feel, not what we ought to say,

Shakespeare concludes at the end of the play. But what is the audience's reaction? What has been done to it? And how does that compare with what the audience feels emotionally about plays like *Saved* or *Who's Afraid of Virginia Woolf?* or the one we glanced at, *Afore Night Come?*

[6] Luke 12:6.

In both cases there is a kind of exhausted peace. In that sense the Theatre of Cruelty does achieve its end. The audience is 'satisfied'. But the nature of the peace differs immensely. After *King Lear* the quietness that comes is that of a conflict resolved, of an issue determined, of an immense struggle with nightmare forces which have at last been overcome. There is at the deepest level a victory of the spirit. This audience involvement in a spiritual struggle of vast implications satisfies a pattern we know within; the force of equal vigour which declares that man and his world is made for good and not evil. (*King Lear* is not a Christian play but its pattern, with the triumph of good after much suffering, is a Christian one.) By contrast, the drama of the Theatre of Cruelty produces a peace which is that of the 'sated' rather than the 'satisfied'. There is no attempt to create a clash of opposing forces where the issue hangs in doubt: rather there is the releasing of all inhibitions in an attempt not to meet the violence but to take part in it, to become one with it, so that all one's energy is released into it, not against it.

The difficulty in this for the Christian is the way such a dramatic experience demands of him an 'acting out' at a deeper than rational level, at that very profound level where the emotions and the imagination become totally engaged, of a pattern of life which in totality is a denial of his relationship with God. For in his daily encounter with hatred, anger and cruelty within himself, his living relationship with God gives him faith in an ultimate victory, not yet wholly seen or perpetually experienced, but trusted in because he trusts in the power of Christ's own victory, once for all time, in the encounter with evil, on his behalf. If he involves himself too deeply, therefore, in a ritualized acting through of passions and violence, he is in danger of denying this trust, because he is taking part in an 'orgy' whose basis is wholly pagan, a crucifixion without any glimpse of a resurrection.

This is not to say that a Christian must not involve himself in the situation of 'man-without-God'. On the contrary, he must, as happens in *Lear*, be so wholly involved in that situation that his involvement speaks aloud of what he understands of the *truth* of life. But for him the 'truth of life' is not a state of defeat by passions and desires, but of Christ's victory over these on his behalf. So his dramatic experience must be an encounter, not a passivity.

Not all writers see the Theatre of Cruelty as being the solution to their problems. There is still the need, felt by many, to find something that is uniquely and unshakably themselves, which, because of its integrity, can combat both the fury of cruelty and the insidious disintegration of spirit which the mid-century knows. And this obviously leads directly to the searching questions which we pinpointed at the beginning of this study as being those in which writers today show their keenest interest: Who am I? What am I? Where am I? How can I know myself? How can I *establish* myself? Is there any 'myself' to know? In what terms can I express that which is myself?

Leaving aside, now, what writers have seen about influences upon ourselves, we come in the next few pages to attempts made in recent years to examine what man's self really is, how it is expressed, and what are some of the problems inevitably involved. The fundamental importance of such inquiries to Christian and non-Christian alike needs no underlining.

5 WHO OR WHAT AM I:
Some experimental answers

> What is the first and most fundamental truth which an incarnate being must realise? That he is a thing, a material object in space and time, and that as such he will come to an end. What is the next …truth which he must realise? That he is related on the one hand to God, who is not a thing, and on the other hand to other things which surround him. Now these other things . . . are some of them mere things, and others of them God related things like himself.[1]

POINTERS TO IDENTITY: I AM ME BECAUSE I REMEMBER

At the beginning of Chapter 2 we listened briefly to two people arguing, as people frequently do, about what day of the week something had happened; and we noted that a good deal of the passion most of us have known in such discussions came from the way each speaker identified herself (I don't know why I imagine them as women!) with her own memory of the event.

Now this idea, that memory is a very personal thing, that in fact it has something to do with our very self, has been explored by some contemporary writers. Nigel Dennis, for instance, has the theory that personal identity is really only the sum of memories and that it can be wiped out just as they can. If this page were impregnated with some secret chemical which had the effect of wiping

[1] Bledyard in Iris Murdoch's *The Sandcastle* (Chatto and Windus, 1957).

out the whole of any reader's memory as he turned to it, so that he did not know his name, where he was sitting, what he was doing there, then, Dennis would argue, his identity would be non-existent and he could be given a new one.

> Because memory is fallible and therefore subject to infinite distortion, so is the personal identity always a false creation, merely the self portrait of a biased, cunning artist. . . . The prime demonstrable point of this discovery is that a man so rests upon his memories that he can be changed almost out of recognition if these memories can be edited, if new memories can be put in the place of old ones.[2]

So he wrote *Cards of Identity*, a novel later dramatized, to examine this concept from several angles. It was possible, he suggested, to make a character behave according to a completely different set of rules by giving him a new set of memories. The psychological theories behind this are fairly obvious. The interesting thing is that this notion—which is by no means new—had in fact been presented from an exactly opposite viewpoint in 1943 by Graham Greene in *The Ministry of Fear*,[3] a spy story where the central character is brainwashed of all his memories and given a new formal identity *in order* to change his loyalties and make him work for 'the enemy'. But Greene makes his hero accept this to the point where the situation he is in calls for a moral judgment, and then something other than his pseudo-memory asserts itself and he acts in accord with those values which had been shown to be his at the beginning of the story.

I AM ME BECAUSE I BELIEVE IN . . .

Greene is arguing, in fact, that name and clothes and even substitute memories do not alter those values which a man has made so completely his own that they have become part of himself. It is these, the causes for which he will die, Greene urges, that give a man meaning as a human being and identity as an individual.

John Le Carré makes a similar point in *The Spy who Came*

[2] Preface to *Cards of Identity* (Weidenfeld and Nicolson, 1955).
[3] Heinemann, 1943 and 1960.

in from the Cold,[4] but in a different way. In this book Leamas, the British agent, lacks a philosophy on which his life is based, and this contributes to the 'ghost-like' sense of himself from which he suffers. Here he is being questioned by a Communist agent about the philosophy which motivates the British Secret Service personnel:

To Leamas, that was the most difficult question of all.

'What do you mean, a philosophy?' he replied, 'we're not Marxists, we're nothing. Just people.'

'Are you Christians, then?'

'Not many, I shouldn't think. I don't know many.'

'What makes them do it, then? . . . They must have a philosophy.'

'Why must they? Perhaps they don't know; don't even care. Not everyone has a philosophy', Leamas answered, a little helplessly...

'But what is the justification, then? What is it? For us it is easy, as I said to you last night. . . . Then what do you think? What is your philosophy?'

'I just think the whole lot of you are bastards.'. . .

'And that justifies, for instance, the taking of human life? That justifies the bomb in the crowded restaurant; that justifies your write-off of agents—all that? . . .

'I don't know', Leamas said. He added, 'I don't much care.'

This idea is developed by many writers who locate who a man is in his sense of certain values which he can never surrender. But, as we shall see, this theme leads us into one of the most complex and agonizing of present-day problems.

To begin, however, let us look at a clear and straightforward exposition of a man defining himself by what he believes in and acts on. Robert Bolt conceives (not necessarily with historical accuracy) of Sir Thomas More in precisely these terms and says so in his preface to the play *A Man for all Seasons*.[5]

At any rate, Sir Thomas More, as I wrote about him, became for me a man with an adamantine sense of his own self. He knew where he began and left off, what area of himself he could yield to the encroachments of his enemies, and what to the encroachments of those he loved. . . . At length he was asked to retreat from that final area where he located his self. And there the supple, humorous,

[4] Gollancz, 1963.   [5] Heinemann, 1960.

unassuming and sophisticated person set like metal, was overthrown by an absolutely primitive rigour and could no more be budged than a cliff . . . What first attracted me was a person who could not be accused of any incapacity for life, who indeed seized life in a great variety, who nevertheless found something in his self without which life was valueless and when that was denied him was able to grasp his death.

Robert Bolt is not, by his own declaration, a Christian. But what he has done here is to enter into a human being's need for commitment to some cause, something outside himself, before he can realize *himself* as a human being. And it so happens that the example he chose was of a man involved in the deepest kind of commitment, commitment to the Christian faith. He is therefore implying what, as we showed earlier, a Christian will assert, that values are not variable and ephemeral according to one's feelings and whims, but that they are objective. One can identify oneself with them, make them in a way part of oneself, yet they remain external and so can be clung to when all else fails. And they provide man with an identity, a cause to die for.

So, not surprisingly, Bolt's central figure makes upon the audience a tremendous impact as a real person, a person with a recognizable identity. There is no disintegration, either sudden or insidious, here:

> I neither could nor would rule my king . . . but there's a little . . . little . . . area . . . where I must rule myself. It's a very little—less to him than a tennis court.

And so even under pressure his prayer is, 'I make my petition to Almighty God that He will keep me in this my honest mind to the last hour that I shall live.'

I AM ME BECAUSE I DO

Other writers carry on this idea in more concrete terms when they use a man's work to epitomize his sense of value, although in fact this happens more rarely, as we shall see later. R. S. Thomas's poem 'Schoonermen'[6] does this.

[6] In *Pieta* (Rupert Hart-Davis, 1967).

Great in this
They made small ships do
Big things, leaping hurdles
Of the stiff sea, horse against horses
In the tide race.

> What has Rio
To do with Pwllheli? Ask winds
Bitter for ever
With their black shag. Ask the quays
Stained with spittle.

> Four days out
With bad cargo
Fever took the crew;
The mate and boatswain
Peering in turn
Through the spray's window,
Brought her home. Memory aches
In the bones' rigging. If tales were tall,
Waves were taller.

> From long years
In a salt school, caned by brine,
They came landward
With the eyes of boys,
The Welsh accent
Thick in their sails.

Many of his poems on Welsh farm life and the slow cycle of its activity have the same theme, and so does much of Norman Nicholson's work.

I AM ME BECAUSE I ENJOY

Much more widely used in English literature, however, is the sense of the value of cultural discovery, of a world of beauty which makes the person and place mean something. Beattie in Arnold Wesker's *Roots*,[7] for instance, cries out as she listens to Bizet's 'L'Arlésienne' suite,

[7] In *Wesker Trilogy* (Cape, 1960).

62

Listen, listen, it goes together, the two tunes together. They knit, they're perfect. Don't it make you want to dance? Listen to that, Mother. . . . It's light. It makes me feel light and confident and happy. God, Mother, we could all be so much more happy and alive. Wheee!!

This is no mere hedonism, no selfish indulgence in pleasure. Its essence is selflessness, unselfconsciousness. It is what C. S. Lewis has called 'pure joy'. And by grasping hold of this external value—in this case a certain quality in music—and identifying oneself with it, some writers would assert, one is able to define one's self.

John Osborne explores a similar idea in *The Entertainer*:[8]

Did I ever tell you the most moving thing I ever heard? It was when I was in Canada—I managed to slip over the border sometimes to some people I knew, and one night I heard some negress singing in a bar. *Now you're going to smile at this*, you're going to smile your educated English head off. . . . If ever I saw any hope or strength in the human race it was in the face of that old, fat negress getting up to sing about Jesus or something like that. She was poor and lonely and repressed like nobody you've ever known. Or me, for that matter. I never even liked that kind of music, but to see that old black whore singing her heart out to the whole world, you knew somehow in your heart it didn't matter how much you kick people, the real people, how much you despise them, if they can stand up and make a pure, just natural noise like that, there's nothing wrong with them, only with everybody else. I've never heard anything like that since. . . . If I'd done one thing as good as that in my whole life, I'd have been all right.

It is Archie Rice speaking, the broken-down music-hall comedian. His one moment of genuine identity comes when the news is broken to him that his soldier son, Mick, hourly expected home, has been killed. He sits at the table without moving and out of the pure depth of grief sings very slowly a blues song. At that moment Osborne conceives of him, as Arthur Miller says of another figure, as 'himself purely'.

[8] Faber and Faber, 1961.

But having a value which gives meaning to life, having a cause to die for, does not necessarily determine the man, give him shape, identity. It can do the very opposite, break him, reduce him. The reason for this may be seen by considering some of William Golding's work, for he made the subject his particular study in *Pincher Martin*,[9] and in *The Spire*[1] where it is more subtly expressed. John Braine, too, shows the effects of a man's adherence to the wrong kind of values in his job.

Pincher Martin's consuming value, the motive which is his basis, is self-preservation. It has been so all his life and is at the moment Golding describes when he is contesting a death by drowning. He is fighting not merely drowning but annihilation as a person. But to the struggle he can bring only those negative values which have governed his life, his petty hates and jealousies of his rival and his desires to possess material success and his girlfriend. Because these have no positive virtue, Golding suggests, Pincher Martin is washed out, obliterated.

A similar realization comes to Joe Lampton in John Braine's *Room at the Top*[2] and *Life at the Top*.[3] He abandons the woman he loved simply in order to make a useful marriage which will take him further in his career, and the woman he had abandoned kills herself. It is then that he sees that he has lost himself; a stranger lives in his skin:

> I didn't like Joe Lampton. He was a sensible young accountant with a neatly pressed suit and a stiff white collar. He always said and did the right thing and never embarrassed anyone with an unseemly display of emotion. . . . I hated Joe Lampton, but he looked and sounded very sure of himself, sitting at my desk in my skin; he'd come to stay, this was no flying visit.[4]

This analysis of what matters to a man and how far it can withstand pressure, at what point it—and therefore the man—breaks,

---

[9] Faber and Faber, 1956.
[2] Eyre and Spottiswoode, 1957.
[4] From *Room at the Top*.
[1] Faber and Faber, 1964.
[3] Eyre and Spottiswoode, 1962.

is one of William Golding's key themes. It lies behind *Free Fall*,[5] but it is perhaps most explicitly and vividly expressed in *The Spire*. In this novel, Jocelyn, the central figure, has lofty dreams of service to God and the community, symbolized in the building of a spire on the shaky foundations of a marshland cathedral.

To this end he bends everything he possesses, gives all he has, his time, intelligence, concentration, physical strength. And he compels from others, as much as he is able, the same devotion to the cause. But these visions of service are perverted because they are a subtle expression of his own will to dominate, his own egoism, his own blind spiritual pride. And so the spire of his dreams becomes in actuality a crazy, ramshackle affair, built on the suffering, loss and death of others, threatening hourly to fall but not yet having done so. It is in the horrifying recognition of this that Jocelyn comes to some sort of obedience to Something or Someone beyond himself.

So we have come back to the assertion made at the beginning, that man needs some external values, some cause to die for, to give his life significance. Golding stresses, though in humanistic terms, the paradox that the Christian understands, that who puts selfish desires first loses his precious 'self'. Kingsley Amis summarized it:

> By yielding mastery the will is freed,
> For it is by surrender that we live,
> And we are taken if we wish to give,
> Are needed if we need.[6]

But Golding has also revealed one of the deep problems expressed by modern writers of this idea of locating the self in values. For he has shown that man can delude himself and choose the wrong values. He is changeable, full of doubts and self-questionings. How can he be certain that his motives are right, that he has not chosen values which will lead to his destruction?

This is a danger that Christians need to be particularly aware of and honest about. Aware of the doubts and self-questionings which, at least at a superficial level, torment all of us, however deep our knowledge of God's love, we understand why some

[5] Faber and Faber, 1960.

[6] Kingsley Amis, 'Masters', *A Case of Samples* (Gollancz, 1965).

writers assert the impossibility of any man being certain of his own commitment. The confidence of the Christian lies not at all in himself but in his knowledge that the God to whom he has committed himself, who is both infinite and personal, is fully able to keep him in all circumstances, however weak and uncertain he knows himself to be. Perhaps one of the best illustrations of this in modern terms is to be found in Dietrich Bonhoeffer's poem 'Who am I?'[7] in which he speaks openly of the impression of unshakability he gives to others, of his private knowledge of his own sick doubts and fears, and of his absolute certainty of God's grip on his life:

> Who am I? They often tell me
> I would step from my cell's confinement
> calmly, cheerfully, firmly,
> like a squire from his country-house.
> Who am I? They often tell me
> I would talk to my warders
> freely and friendly and clearly,
> as though it were mine to command.
> Who am I? They also tell me
> I would bear the days of misfortune
> equably, smilingly, proudly,
> like one accustomed to win.
>
> Am I then really all that which other men tell of?
> Or am I only what I myself know of myself,
> restless and longing and sick, like a bird in a cage,
> struggling for breath, as though hands were compressing my throat,
> yearning for colours, for flowers, for the voices of birds,
> thirsting for words of kindness, for neighbourliness,
> tossing in expectation of great events,
> powerlessly trembling for friends at an infinite distance,
> weary and empty at praying, at thinking, at making,
> faint, and ready to say farewell to it all?
>
> Who am I? This or the other?
> Am I one person today and tomorrow another?
> Am I both at once? A hypocrite before others,
> and before myself a contemptibly woebegone weakling?

[7] In *Letters and Papers from Prison*.

Or is something within me still like a beaten army,
fleeing in disorder from victory already achieved?
Who am I? They mock me, these lonely questions of mine,
Whoever I am, thou knowest, O God, I am thine!

What Bonhoeffer is saying, Paul had already said: 'For I know whom I have believed, and I am sure that he is able to guard until that Day what I have entrusted to him.'[8]

SUPPOSE NO VALUES EXIST?

Not all writers can be as positive as Bonhoeffer. This sense that man can delude himself about his commitment to certain values, this feeling of uncertainty, has led many authors to echo John Osborne's cry in *Look Back in Anger*,[9] that there are no causes left to die for, that no values exist. He is not in fact denigrating the desire of man to attach himself to a cause. Far from it. 'How I long', he makes his hero say, 'How I long for a little ordinary human enthusiasm. Just enthusiasm—that's all. I want to hear a warm, thrilling voice cry out Hallelujah! Hallelujah! I'm alive!' Indeed, for him too it is the secret of being human, of proper human identity:

> I've an idea. Why don't we have a little game? Let's pretend we're human beings and that we're actually alive. Just for a while ... Let's pretend we're human. Oh brother, it's such a long time since I was with anyone who got enthusiastic about anything.

John Osborne's Jimmy Porter is attacking here all those who will not commit themselves and are thus, in a sense, sub-human. But in his cry that there are no causes left to die for there is more than an attack on ourselves. There is a protest against the view that the *universe* seems to make every cause questionable, that for so many writers it has a huge question mark at its centre. No man can commit himself to a cause that does not exist: and if one believes that there is no cause, because there is no pattern or reason in the universe, then self-commitment is not only pointless and futile but dishonest.

[8] 2 Timothy 1:12.   [9] Faber and Faber, 1957.

This sense of the absurdity in life is a widespread one today. Camus, in his early days, was its prophet; Ionesco, Beckett, Pinter, Adamov, Arrabal and many others its dramatic exponents. John Cruikshank has well summarized the essentials of this philosophy: there are 'those experiences that defy rational explanation or seem to confound and controvert our sense of fair play, our desire for happiness, our need to find pattern and purpose in existence'.[1] He includes among the evidence for such contradiction the deadening routine of much industrial life, the sense that 'time is rapidly and inexorably bearing us towards physical disintegration; the consciousness of our brief human lives in contrast to the endurance of inanimate nature; the "otherness" of people and even of an element in ourselves; the waste of so much human potential in apparently arbitrary sudden death or protracted suffering'.

'Men die', Caligula says in Camus's early play, 'and they are not happy. . . . Men weep because . . . the world's all wrong.'[2] It is this sense of tragedy, as Raymond Williams has well pointed out,[3] that connects the three characteristically new systems of thinking in our own time, Marxism, Freudianism and Existentialism. Marxism sees man as achieving his full life only after violent conflict. For Freudianism 'man is essentially frustrated and divided against himself while he lives in society'. Williams comments that existentialist man is torn 'by intolerable contradictions in a condition of essential absurdity. . . . From these ordinary propositions and from their combination in so many minds it is not surprising that so much tragedy has, in fact, emerged.' It is for this reason that one can link John Osborne's cry of pain and longing and Camus's sense of despair in his early work. Violence and frustration are their context: and from them have come not only the Theatre of Protest and the Theatre of the Absurd (at which we shall be looking more closely later), but the Theatre of Cruelty.

[1] John Cruikshank, Introduction to Camus's *Caligula* and *Cross Purpose* (Penguin Plays, 1965).

[2] *Caligula*, trans. Stuart Gilbert (Hamish Hamilton, 1948).

[3] 'Tragic Despair and Revolt', *Critical Quarterly*, Vol. 5, No. 2 (Summer 1963).

Sartre and Camus are very closely linked in spite of their famous
quarrel and so we must glance, though briefly here, at Sartre's
Existentialism. For again its mood, although not necessarily its
systematized thinking, has its effect on a wide range of English
writers. For when John Osborne demanded 'enthusiasm', he was
in fact expressing one aspect of existentialist thought, that 'authentic
existence' (or, to avoid the jargon, being 'fully alive') is achieved
only in action and encounter.

Sartre defines the essence of man as his 'freedom', by which he
means a 'nothingness' with which one begins and the necessity
of determining for oneself what is of value and what is not. Through
this choosing, Sartre argues, each individual creates both himself
and his world. 'For human reality to be is to choose one's self.' So
man makes himself and his own realm; there is no 'universe'.
'Values are not recognized by man but determined by him: I am
the being by whom values exist.' But man achieves this identity
only if he *exercises* his freedom. If he does not exercise it, he does
not 'create himself'.

Sartre goes on to examine the religious and moral implications
of this exercise, as he sees them. In relation to religion, he argues
that the essentially human characteristic of 'emptiness' (= freedom)
is balanced by everyone's attempt to be the opposite of empty,
'solid' through and through. And this is an impossibility. In his
lecture *Existentialism and Humanism*[4] he explained why. *Pour-soi*, he
said, meant a consciousness of one's consciousness; *l'en-soi* means
to be absolute, to be 'solid', to be so much oneself that there is no
rift in oneself and one is not conscious of oneself. The fundamental
drive of religion is towards a fusion of the two, in transcendental
terms, and this fusion *pour-soi-l'en-soi* raised to infinity is God.
But this attempted fusion is by definition doomed to frustration;
and so there can be no God, since the notion is self-contradictory.
Thus, Sartre says, 'every human reality is a passion in that it projects
losing itself. . . . But the idea of God is contradictory and we lose
ourselves in vain. Man is a useless passion.'

[4] Trans. P. Mairet (Methuen, 1948).

In moral terms two elements appear. One is the danger of adopting other people's values instead of knowingly and consciously determining one's own; this is 'bad faith' in Sartre's terms, since it evades our freedom. As Mary Warnock[5] points out, this kind of morality, while not unattractive, is entirely negative. It simply means, in the attempt to isolate oneself, 'to escape the influence of one's environment and heroically to take full responsibility for what it is one does'. More positively, Sartre insists on man's realizing his freedom through action, not as a dispassionate spectator but as an actor within a concrete situation surrounded by other people, involved therefore in decision. This action will find its shape in encounter with people.

Depressingly in this encounter Sartre sees only three possible modes of action. We tend to treat all other people as 'things', not as people with the same freedom as ourselves, because their freedom threatens ours. Yet we want to possess the *person*; and what makes that person, gives 'it' humanity, is its freedom to love back or reject, to think and plan for itself. Therefore, Sartre argues, we shall either surrender the attempt and resume indifference, or we may turn to masochism (aiming to become a thing ourselves, to be used and controlled by the other), or we may attempt violence upon the other, to possess by storm, reducing it thereby to a 'thing'. Sartre has a horrifying consciousness of the hostility of 'things'—*i.e.* of the material world— caught in *Nausea*, where the symbol of syrupy stickiness seems to him to epitomize the 'otherness' and 'estrangement' of the material universe we find ourselves in.

I have spent some little time on this because, as will shortly appear, fragments of these ideas, developments of this mood, appear in a good number of English books of the mid-century. We shall be looking in more detail in Chapter 7 at some of the Christian evaluations of Existentialism (which, it must be understood, is a very loosely-knit collection of ideas propounded by many thinkers). But I think we might note in passing one of the chief objections to Existentialism carried to its logical conclusion, which was voiced by George Chapman when he said,

[5] *Existentialist Ethics* (Macmillan, 1967).

> Shall I think the complete universe must be
> Subject to such a rag of it as me?[6]

In Christian terms one of the main limitations of existential thought is that, while it demands decision in encounter and in action, it is in fact viewing this encounter and action only in terms of the individual; all the activity is implicitly his. This has two implications. First, as we saw above, it means that, to each individual, other people are reduced to the status of 'things'. It follows from this that any personal, two-way encounter between human beings is impossible and, similarly, that the notion of encounter with a personal God, initiated by Him, is inconceivable. The idea of 'the spirit blows where it wills', of 'God was in Christ' who said 'My Father is working still and I am working', this urgent activity of God both from His side of the encounter and also prompting and directing individuals, is wholly lost.

Secondly there is the danger of limiting humanity's range. It is the individual, and not any other member of the human race, who in his own view counts: he determines his own values, his own ethical code, if he has one. There is no room at all for objectivity, whether humanist or transcendent. The system is so narrow that it is not even man who becomes the measure of all things, man at his most exciting and best: it is this diminutive, limited example of man that is me.

THE APE AND THE MAN IN CHAOS

We must return here to the effect of this on English literature. One notable writer in 1956, Colin Wilson, adopting the title of Camus's 1942 novel *The Outsider*, expounded many of the ideas briefly summarized above.[7] The first point he makes is the existentialist one that the moment is gone for ever, that the past does not live on, that memory falsifies and cannot repeat in actuality the experience it codes. We fabricate details in order to attempt to re-create, in

[6] In 'Knell', from *Drink from the Rock*, quoted by Charles Williams in *War in Heaven* (Faber and Faber, 1962).

[7] Colin Wilson, *The Outsider* (Gollancz, 1956). See also *Beyond the Outsider* (Arthur Barker, 1965).

imagination, the vitality of the incident. (Note how this is the direct contradiction of the theory of self with which we began this chapter.) Secondly, he isolates the attempts men make to gloss over the savage and irrational within them by their respectability and philosophy. To stand for truth in such things is to be an Outsider:

> The ape and the man exist in one body; and when the ape's desires are about to be fulfilled, he disappears and is succeeded by the man, who is disgusted with the ape's appetites. This is the problem of the Outsider. . . .

Wilson goes on from there to expound the central thesis of absurdity:

> The Outsider is a man who cannot live in the comfortable, insulated world of the bourgeois, accepting what he sees and touches as reality. 'He sees too deep and too much' and what he sees is essentially *chaos* . . . The world is not rational, not orderly. When he asserts his sense of anarchy in the face of the bourgeois' complacent acceptance, it is not merely the need to cock a snook at respectability that provokes him; it is a distressing sense *that truth must be told at all costs*. Even if there seems no room for hope, truth must be told. . . . The Outsider is a man who has awakened to chaos.

It is the air of discovery with which this is asserted which is perhaps most moving. Most of it is true, of course. We do all know 'the ape and the man within'. The happy liberalism of the progressive evolutionist is built on a blindness to the Belsen within each of us, a Belsen where we are both guard and prisoner. But again this is no new thought. 'For I do not do what I want, but I do the very thing I hate', said Paul.[8] 'Jesus', John recorded,[9] 'did not trust himself to them . . . for he himself knew what was in man.'

Man's complacency may need to be shattered, but the final truth is not of the despair of the Outsider, but the hope of the Insider. The truth must indeed be told at all costs, but it includes not only Herod's slaughter of the Innocents but a cradle, not only

[8] Romans 7:15. [9] John 2:24.

a flogging and an execution but an empty tomb and a mountain.[1]

The relevance of Wilson's work to playwrights like John Osborne and Harold Pinter is fairly clear, and we shall be looking in detail at a play by Pinter at the end of this chapter and noticing how it picks up some of these ideas and extends them dramatically. What we must spend time on now is, first, the development of the idea of the escape from man's apparent predicament into hedonism and the reaction against this which is now occurring, and, second, the development from it of the Theatre of the Absurd, and a further notable development in thinking which came from that.

ESCAPE INTO PLEASURE?

If life is chaotic and absurd, then 'let us eat, drink and be merry'. One of the implications of the 'Absurd' in action is the collapse of ethical structure. It is this which John Osborne analyses in his play *A Bond Honoured*[2] in which he examines what happened to an individual who makes pleasure his only value. 'Pleasure' is here stretched to involve any kind of perversion as well as the more generally understood levels of its meaning. Leonido, in whom this pattern is worked out, is made to express his motivation quite clearly at the beginning of the play:

> I don't know what virtue is. Can you tell me? I've never had any myself and I've never observed any in others either. . . . You see, there, it all flies back to *pleasure*, like stooping falcon. Pleasure in self, shallow self, cracked and wormy as I may be. . . . Good and evil are men's opinions of themselves.

But haunting him throughout his career is his sense that there may be a debt to pay for this pleasure, a bond to be honoured. 'Remember:' Tizon says to him, 'you have a debt to pay to heaven. . . .'

---

[1] It involves, in explicit theological terms, agreeing that man is full of 'all manner of wickedness, evil, covetousness, malice, . . . envy, murder, strife, deceit . . .' (Romans 1:29). But it includes also the confident assertion that 'for our sake he made him to be sin who knew no sin, so that in him we might become the righteousness of God' (2 Corinthians 5:21). Man is not only a fallen hero, but a redeemed one.

[2] Faber and Faber, 1966.

Gradually Leonido 'feels the bond tightening'. What Obsorne asserts in the play is the belief that man's very nature demands of him a debt: because he is what he is there will be a reckoning. But this is not because of the demands of patriotism nor the assertions of religion. 'I was once dressed as a Sicilian. Christian. But neither Sicilian nor Christian meant anything to me.' Nationality and religious creed are both merely 'a dress' for Osborne. What he is aiming at is what we would call the essential man *under* the dress; and here he deliberately uses the words of St Paul to express the pattern he sees.

VOICE: For that which I do.
LEONIDO: I allow not. For what I would, that I do not. But what I hate: that I do. I know that in me.
VOICE: In my flesh.
LEONIDO: There is no good thing. For the will is present in me. But how to perform what is good. I find . . .
VOICE: Not.
LEONIDO: For the good thing I would, I do not . . . But the evil: that I do. So then I find the law. When I do good evil is present in me. For I delight in the law of God in the inward man. But I see another law in my members warring against the law of my mind, and bringing me into captivity.
VOICE: To the law of sin.
LEONIDO: Which of my members? Who shall deliver me?

The shepherd who enters gives Leonido a 'meagre pouch' which contains the debt he owes 'which must be recovered'. It contains

. . . . A crown. I shall wear that . . . A tunic. Oh yes. And with lash marks on it. It looks like a motto, is it your motto, some device? . . . What else is there? A rope. That's good . . . What are these things? More clothes.
(He takes out a cross.)
Why are you mocking me? If you were God Himself you'd get no reprieve from me. . . . I am going to kill you.
(He falls to the ground.)
SHEPHERD: What are you afraid of, Leonido?

The play, of course, is not a Christian play. We must not be mesmerized into thinking it is. It uses Christian imagery and it makes part of the Christian assertion. But, like his play *Luther*, it flirts with Christianity and then evades it. Leonido is hanged, having given himself up, at the end of the play. And the final comment on him is,

> Well . . . he played a good tune on vituperation. It may not be a bond honoured, but it's a tune of sorts to end with.

It is not a Christian play because it leaves out the Godward end of the debt. It sees the debt as rooted in man's nature but not—except in a muddled, incomplete way—as God's concern. And certainly the honouring of the bond is not through God's effectiveness. Vituperation, not justice or mercy, not compassion or lovingkindness, is its keynote.

Yet it does face the implications of absurdity and the hedonism that follows, and it does face squarely man's nature. This is by no means an isolated instance of the movement against hedonism, a rejection of pleasure as the ultimate end.

A totally different play at a very different level, John Mortimer's *Two Stars for Comfort*,[3] does exactly the same thing. His heroine Ann Martin is trying desperately to prove to herself that she exists, which life in the anonymity of the lodging house has made her doubt. When Sam, the proprietor of the river-side hotel, sees this, he tries to give her identity through pleasure; that is, literally, through *pleasing*. But to do it he falsifies what is true, tells her what she wishes to hear and not what is, in fact, the case. And this is inadequate. The licence of the hotel is withdrawn in the same way that her ability to live in an illusion fades. And Sam, understanding at last what has been wrong, tells the truth. This is an attack on a more subtle form of hedonism, that of the pleasure of giving pleasure to others at the expense of truth. It is insisting—though without the only fundamental basis that makes the act possible—on 'speaking the truth in love'.

[3] Methuen, 1962.

Two Stars for Comfort, while modern in idiom and rhythm, retains
something of the traditional dramatic pattern in its exposition of a
situation through the development of plot. But the Theatre of the
Absurd abandons such traditional dramatic framework (just as
James Joyce abandoned the traditional framework of the novel)
in order to establish what Martin Esslin[4] calls 'a psychological and
inner realism'. Rather than concentrate on the externals of human
existence, dramatists of the Absurd concentrate on the conversation
beneath the conversation, the event below its outer circumstance.
And if for these writers the 'inwardness' of life is chaotic, meaningless, then the pattern of their plays will be also. For such writers
'ultimately man is alone in a meaningless world'. To face such an
idea and to shed what Esslin calls 'comforting illusions, easy
solutions', gives a sense of freedom and relief.

The Theatre of the Absurd, therefore, does not offer the escapism
of hedonism, but faces man's situation. Hence, argues Esslin, it
'does not provoke tears of despair but the laughter of liberation'.
It does provoke laughter; it is often extremely funny. But the laughter
is more complex than Esslin here allows. For there *is* an absurdity
about human beings, particularly when they assume stances and
poses, but it arises not from 'the ultimate meaninglessness of the
universe' but, in fact, from the gesturing of humanity itself. Some
writers of the Absurd catch this. N. F. Simpson does, for instance,
in *A Resounding Tinkle*[5] with his ridiculous but recognizable drama
critics, Salt, Pepper, Mustard and Vinegar. So does Samuel
Beckett with his tramps who move one to laughter and tears at the
same moment, in their exact recapturing of nuances of ordinary,
muddled, wistful conversation.

Samuel Beckett (who must have a brief mention here, although
his inclusion in a book about English literature is questionable,
since he is an Irishman writing in French) is interesting in *Waiting
for Godot*[6] for another reason. His tramps mirror human existence,

---

[4] Introduction to *Absurd Drama* (Penguin, 1965). See also Martin
Esslin, *Theatre of the Absurd* (Eyre and Spottiswoode, 1962).

[5] Faber and Faber, 1958; Penguin, 1960.   [6] Faber and Faber, 1955.

waiting for something to happen, to make all plain, to transform life. While they wait they pass the time as best they can in dressing, arguing, eating, meeting other people, sleeping, quarrelling, playing games, arguing some more. And time and again they return in all these activities to the desire to establish some *facts*, some verifiable, objective, indisputable facts, which will give them a foothold in the universe.

They try to establish definitely what day it was on which they were to meet Godot; they try to ascertain that the two people they meet in the second act were the ones they met in the first, that this was the same place, that these were their own clothes, that the messenger was the same messenger. They attempt to establish certainty through the senses, touching, smelling; through their memories; through reasoning (they debate, for instance, discrepancies in the Gospel account of the crucifixion of the thieves with Jesus, and how certainty can be achieved about it). They attempt, finally, to establish certainty about their own existence.[7]

Now this desire for the certainty and reassurance of fact, the indisputable and unshakable, is the natural recourse of minds shaken by the glimpse of the abyss into which the universe and our private individual worlds seem to be spinning. L. P. Hartley describes precisely the same process in *The Go-Between*[8] in his child, bruised beyond bearing by the encounter with adults who had used him and exposed him to their own mutual, powerful passions:

> But another world came to my aid—the world of facts. I accumulated facts: facts which existed independently of me, facts which I could not add to or subtract from.

[7] Martin Esslin, reviewing *No's Knife*, Beckett's collection of shorter prose, pointed out Beckett's fundamental preoccupation with the essence of Self-hood: 'In each of these the "I" who speaks descends to deeper levels of introspection in an eternal search for the real nature of the Self, an unending quest for non-being or of "ceasing, better still, before having been". This, it must be stressed, is not nihilism or pure negation. It is the quest of all the great mystics of history from Buddha to Master Eckhard and St. John of the Cross' (*Sunday Telegraph*, 16 July, 1967).

[8] Hamish Hamilton, 1953.

L. P. Hartley goes on to point out the danger of 'facts' taking the place of 'truths', the life of facts taking the place of the facts of life; and this is a warning worth heeding. But he is certainly right to show the flight to fact from an overdose of subjectivity. It is a healthy instinct in man which makes him redress the balance by turning to something existing independent of himself which he cannot add to or subtract from. For we cannot be satisfied with a purely subjective world. The Christian knowledge that there are values which exist independently of man's acceptance of them implies, too, the necessity of establishing fact. For the Christian, experience of God is not only a subjective one. It has reference beyond the subjective to the verifiable fact of the incarnation. At such a time, in such a place—fact!—God intervened in the affairs of the world: Christ, the Son of God, was a man in the time of Augustus and Tiberius Caesar.[9] God intervened in the affairs of the world: a God who is apprehensible in terms of encounter, but not definable in those terms. A God who exists in relation to me, but also exists far above and beyond me, and who has existed, does and will exist, whether I had been or not.

[9] Those who are sceptical about the *historical* basis of Christianity, or who have never considered the evidence for it, should read F. F. Bruce, *The New Testament Documents* (IVP, 1960) or Michael Green, *Runaway World*, Chapter 1 (IVP, 1968). And see Bonhoeffer's splendidly simple affirmation: 'In Jesus God has said Yes and Amen to it all, and that Yes and Amen is the firm ground on which we stand. In these turbulent times we repeatedly lose sight of what really makes life worth living. We think that, because this or that person is living, it makes sense for us to live too. But the truth is that if this earth was good enough for the man Jesus Christ, if such a man as Jesus lived, then, and only then, has life a meaning for us. If Jesus had not lived, then our life would be meaningless, in spite of all the other people whom we know and honour and love' *(Letters and Papers from Prison)*.

6 IDENTITY THROUGH OTHERS
A kind of hoping

We have seen that many authors locate a man's identity in something external to himself, whether an abstract value, or something more concrete, such as work. Most frequently, though, authors use relationships as the means of expressing identity, and this is not surprising, since, apart from the inescapable corporateness of the human race we noted in Chapter 1, relationships are what people value most. It is not only that I value my father, my friend, my brother, but that through them I locate something of who I am myself. Relationships, therefore, their nuances and complexities, their ambiguities and paradoxes, have always been the concern of writers, but never more so than now when the self is lonely and longs to hear itself affirmed by the love of others. Terry asks in *Talking to a Stranger*:

> Why is it so lonely? . . . I want to live in a crowd of ten thousand —and never let one of them go home. I want them round me, all round me—day and night—loving me.

THROUGH FAMILY RELATIONSHIPS

Some writers go back to the fundamental blood relationship and explore the meaning which that gives to the individual. Peter Redgrove, for instance, has several poems on this theme, but none, I think, more moving than 'The Archaeologist'.[1]

[1] In *The Collector and Other Poems* (Routledge, 1960).

So I take one of those thin plates
And fit it to a knuckled other,
Carefully, for it trembles on the edge of powder,
Restore the jaw and find the fangs their mates. . . .

I roll the warm wax with my palm
And to the bone slowly mould a face
of the jutting-jawed, hang-browed race;
On the brute strength I try to build up a calm,

For it is a woman, by the broad hips;
I give her a smooth skin, and make the mouth mild:
It is aeons since she saw her child
Spinning thin winds of gossamer from his lips.

This long-dead figure has an identity for us because once she was a mother. For we project into her what we know of the parent-child relationship, a relationship which remains unchanged at its most basic level whatever changes may take place in civilization.[2]

Jon Stallworthy takes this parent-child significance further, suggesting that it is not only the growing child who takes his identity from the parent, but that the parent takes identity from the child. The parent learns not only of self through the relationship, but something more of the meaning of life for that self through the protective pain felt, for instance, for a defective child:

In the days we have known one another,
my little mongol love,
I have learnt more from your lips
than you will from mine perhaps:
I have learned that to live is to suffer
to suffer is to live.[3]

So the fundamental relationship of blood is reaffirmed as of vital importance in discovering one's self.

[2] See also David Holbrook's poem, 'Baby in an Alien Night', *Object Relations* (Methuen, 1967), which expresses the same sense of meaning and definition given to life through the parent-child relationship.

[3] From Jon Stallworthy, 'The Almond Tree', *Poetry 1967* (Critical Quarterly Poetry Supplement No. 8).

Other writers trace how the growing child takes shape as a person from the contacts he has with his fellows and with those adults he necessarily encounters, at whose mercy he stands. The book I mentioned earlier, L. P. Hartley's *The Go-Between*, does just this, as does his earlier trilogy, *Eustace and Hilda*.[4]

An entirely different book, which includes among many others this same theme, is Iris Murdoch's *An Unofficial Rose*,[5] where she creates most delicately the feelings of a little girl in love changing imperceptibly to the emotions of a woman. Miranda has been in love with Felix as long as she can remember; she does not know at what moment her 'childish adoration of that tall gentle-spoken demi-God' had become the 'possessive, jealous agony' that was now her constant preoccupation. At some point her love had been 'set on fire' and now she could not escape. 'In those flames she writhed.' She had suffered as a child in her adoration for him:

> But at least as a child she had not conceived of possessing him. The terrible pain began when, at some half-noticed turning of the way, she found herself in the same world as Felix. For now that nothing separated them, everything separated them.

What is positive about Iris Murdoch's presentation of this situation is its awareness of the child's suffering through the blindness of others. The Felix with whom Miranda is in love still thinks of her as a child, and when she sprains her ankle he brings her— out of a genuinely kind and completely insensitive impulse—a doll. Her reaction puzzles him: the expression in her eyes is of a 'dark violence which he could not decipher'. To make the point clearer, Iris Murdoch precedes the gift with Felix's brisk statement to Miranda of his philosophy in life, and Miranda's reply indicates how incapable he is of applying it to the local situation:

> 'You're very young . . . Other people are what matter about life, and that's the best reason why one just can't contract out of it. We are members one of another, as the service says. But perhaps a child can't be expected to understand.'

[4] Putnam, 1958.   [5] Chatto and Windus, 1962.

'Am I a *child*?' said Miranda . . .
'Damn it, of course you are, Miranda!'

In so far as anyone is ever 'guilty' in Iris Murdoch's book, Felix
is guilty. So, it may be said, is Miranda, who because of her
jealous love for Felix deliberately smashes the growing intimacy
between her mother (deserted by husband) and Felix. The result is
a kind of murder—murder of a relationship which might have
become real and never did. It is symbolized by the fate of the doll
Felix gave Miranda which she 'transfixed through the middle
by the German dagger and pinned to the shelf'. It is 'a sinister
little portent'.

There are several things we should note here. The first is Iris
Murdoch's use of the word 'possess' in the first passage quoted,
when speaking of adult relationships between man and woman.
The second is the quotation by Felix, from 'the service', 'we are
members one of another'. And the third is the implication of guilt
and violence arising from a mishandled relationship. I think Iris
Murdoch is right to use the word 'possess' as a shorthand for the
current popular view of the man-woman relationship. And I also
think she is right to set this in antithesis to the Christian view of
relationship 'members one of another', ironically though she does it
in Felix's comment.

For often the mid-century view is that one is in a relationship for
what one gets out of it: the experience helps one to be oneself, to
grow 'mature'; and this is really the main thing about it. Hence,
once the relationship ceases to seem vital, once it seems to one of
the two involved in it to have no further meaning and depth, it is
'right' for the one partner in it to leave the other, whatever the other
might feel. (*An Unofficial Rose* traces this, too.) This is Sartre's
'treating other people as things', this is limiting the human relationship's potential merely to the possessive, because no other is possible.
On this view the only moral crime possible, therefore, in a relationship, is the crime against *oneself*.

RESPONSIBILITY IN LOVE

But this is a very limited view of the possibilities of relationship.
We begin to realize some of the potential of the man-woman

relationship only when we begin to realize what it involves in responsibility for the other person. This is what the Christian's 'being members one of another' implies, or part of what it implies. It is not only that whether we like it or not, all we do and are affects a widening circle of humanity beyond any possible calcula/ tion. We do not only affect others because we have to, because we cannot help ourselves. We are *responsible* in our affecting. Curiously we understand this socially today, as the idea of the Welfare State (and the writing I quoted in Chapter 3) proves. But we do not seem to have understood this in personal, individual, particularly sexual, terms.

Stephen Spender expresses well the moral crime involved in ignoring it:

> Lightly, lightly from my sleep
>   She stole, our vows of dew to break,
> Upon a day of melting rain
>   Another love to take;
> Her happy happy perfidy
> Was justified was justified
> Since compulsive needs of sense
>   Clamour to be satisfied
>   And she was never one to miss
>   The plausible happiness
> Of a new experience.
>
> I, who stand beneath a bitter
>   Blasted tree, with the green life
> Of summer joy cut from my side
>   By that self/justifying knife,
>   In my exiled misery
>   Were justified were justified
> If upon two lives I preyed
>   Or punished with my suicide,
>   Or murdered pity in my heart
>   Or two other lives did part
> To make the world pay what I paid.[6]

[6] From 'Song', *Collected Poems 1928–1953* (Faber and Faber, 1955).

So the dagger and the smashed dolls used in *An Unofficial Rose* are good symbols for the murderous effects of irresponsibility in relationships. We shall be looking at this in further detail when we study Harold Pinter's work, but it must be seen here at this point in its relevance on the one hand to the shaping of the child as it grows and to love between man and woman on the other.

This is not to say that today's writers are unable to delight in the joy and vitality of encounter between man and woman; one of the few joys in today's writing is that of lovers finding each other and themselves at the same time. I would like to mention here a strange little play, a kind of macabre fairy tale, in which David Campton suggests this crystallizing of true individuality through love. Called *Little Brother, Little Sister*,[7] it is set in the future in the closing years of the twentieth century after some undefined world catastrophe. The three characters, Sir, Madam and Cook, have been in an air-raid shelter for up to twenty years.

Sir and Madam, both born in the shelter, are now just discovering their love for each other. Cook, the tyrant of the shelter, tries to deny it as she once denied the possibility of love in her own life:

> There's things best not remembered. Once I 'ad a name besides Cook, but I left it behind. Rememberin' things like that wakes you up in the night. . . . I always 'ad a single bed. None of your Cook/ Chauffeur business for me. I was 'Ead Cook or nothin'.

But the two youngsters finding each other are also finding their true selves in this relationship:

> There's a me inside me. There's a you inside you, but you haven't found him yet. The me inside me isn't afraid. . . .

And they are released by their discovery.

Even more directly, there is the kind of joy Philip Larkin describes in 'Wedding Wind'[8] where the love between the woman and man makes the whole world make sense to them. Edward Thomas, earlier, had put it precisely.

> And you, Helen, what should I give you? . . .
> I would give you back yourself. . . .

[7] Methuen, 1966.
[8] In *The Less Deceived* (Marvell Press, 1955).

And myself, too, if I could find
Where it lay hidden, and it proved kind.[9]

The gift of the lover: to give his love, what she herself is, with himself added. But while this is the dream, the hope, in human relationships, writer after writer maps the difficulties and pain inevitably involved—the cost of it all.

Arnold Wesker traces this beautifully in *The Four Seasons*.[1] At the end of their year together, the man and woman seem helpless to avoid hurting each other. Adam, the man, speaks of how much easier it is to love babies, corpses, scarecrows, than another person because they do not answer back and, 'We all know ourselves don't we? Who needs to be told . . . ?' But corpses and scarecrows don't return love when it is given. 'Only a human being can return that and the price you pay is the advantage they take. That's the hell of it.'

HONESTY IN RELATIONSHIPS

To attempt to avoid this intentional or unintentional hurtfulness, writers demand honesty in relationships. This is seen as essential because without it these relationships will destroy rather than create and reveal the people involved in them. This is one of the things *Look Back in Anger* was about. Samuel Beckett's *Eh Joe*[2] is entirely concerned with this, the single character haunted by, driven to death by, the memory of those he has 'murdered' by his disloyalty and falseness. A play which comes just within our period since it was first produced in 1958 is concerned very deeply with this. *The Elder Statesman*[3] is by T. S. Eliot, a writer we do not normally associate with the contemporary mood at all, since in both idiom and content—apart from mere chronology—he stands for much that mid-century writers reject. But his last play is a manifesto on the nature and meaning of love and in particular an urgent plea for honesty in it.

[9] From 'And you, Helen', *Collected Poems of Edward Thomas* (Ingpen and Grant, 1922).
[1] Jonathan Cape, 1966.
[2] Faber and Faber, 1967.
[3] Faber and Faber, 1959.

He explores the bond between father and son, daughter and father, daughter and fiancé, man and woman, friend and friend, and suggests that lack of honesty in any one of these leads to a lack of honesty with oneself about what one really is, and so falsifies any other relationship in which one is involved. So Lord Claverton, the elder statesman, has a public image which is false because he has never been honest with himself about the disloyalties of his past. He has been untrue to a friend and false to a woman and because of this unacknowledged, unknown treason of the past, his relationships with his wife, his son, even to some extent his daughter, are falsified. Before he can meet death calmly, even with joy and hope, he has to face what has been false and begin again to learn what relationships can teach him.

> I feel at peace now
> It is the peace that ensues upon contrition
> When contrition ensues upon the knowledge of the truth.
> Why did I always want to dominate my children? . . .
> Because I wanted you to give your life to adoring
> The man that I pretended to myself that I was,
> I've only just now had the illumination
> of knowing what love is.

In this frame of mind, Lord Claverton rejoices that his daughter can love her fiancé, Charles, for what he really is. She is able to reply that her love for her father too, now, is for

> The real you . . . the man you are
> Not the man I thought you were.

And Monica and Charles go on to speak of what their love for each other, honest in this way, can create.

> A new person
> Who is you and me together.

They pour out the ecstasy of their pure love for each other in terms which are deliberately Christian:

> Oh my dear,
> I love you to the limits of speech and beyond. . . .
> I've loved you from the beginning of the world

Before you and I were born, the love was always there
That brought us together.

And in this love they turn gratefully to the elder statesman whose
willingness to be 'a beginner in the practice of loving' has released
them from a false situation. 'In becoming no one he has become
himself'. Monica says, 'Only my father now, and Michael's.' For,
hiding no longer behind the masks he had assumed of status and
impregnable virtue, the elder statesman has learned to be honest
about himself and about his needs and those of others in relationships, and because of this he has released the tremendously creative
power of a love that is not self-seeking in all their lives.

Age and decrepitude can have no terrors for me
Loss and vicissitude cannot appal me
Not even death can dismay or amaze me
Fixed in the certainty of love unchanging.

It is on this subject of relationships and our finding our true
selves in them that modern literature is perhaps most perceptive
and has most to teach us. Certainly it is profoundly thought-
provoking. We have already seen in Chapter 2 that there is a
demand for respect for people, simply because they are human:
and valid relationships begin from there. But there is a whole
dimension missing in most writers which people like T. S. Eliot
supply; for Eliot is a Christian author who understands all relationships as finding their true basis finally in that between God and
man. A contemporary song by Sidney Carter perhaps makes one
aspect of this clearer.

When the King of all Creation
Had a cradle on the earth
Holy was the human body
Holy was the human birth . . .

So the blood relationship, the parent-child relationship, *all*
human contacts, have been potentially sanctified by the incarnation
which expressed God's involvement in man and man's involvement
with God. It is this which gives the Christian his direction in
relationships and throws light most clearly on what these relationships can teach him of himself.[4]

[4] See final chapter of this book, for the development of this.

Yet apart from deliberate irresponsibility, we all know what it is to be puzzled by a human relationship, to be aware of sudden changes and insecurities in it, finding suddenly boggy ground under our feet or shifting sand where there had been a firm path. We all know how no relationship is static but continually changing and developing, and most of us have experienced the sense of personal insecurity this can give. For this reason the modern preoccupation with human encounter, in which some writers saw the best possibility of finding oneself, has an adverse side in which other writers are suggesting that in fact it is in relationships that we are most likely to be puzzled about ourselves, because in them nothing is firm and reliable, nothing stable.

One of the most perceptive and able dramatists to express this is Harold Pinter. He is preoccupied with the way in which people change their roles in any relationship, the way in which they become quite different people; and (as in the life he is mirroring) it is difficult to tell whether it is the changing, developing person who is altering the role or the changing role which alters the person. At the heart of the shifting and changing is the attempt to find out the person himself.

Pinter wrote a radio play, *The Dwarfs*,[5] performed in 1960, which is very important to our understanding of what he is trying to do in all his plays. In it he explores two things; our inability to communicate clearly with each other and our sense of guilt concerning the things we know about ourselves. Together these work to create a feeling of menace in which our very self is threatened: and this self is the most important thing there is, the point of it all.

> The point is, who are you? Not why or how, not even what. I can see what, perhaps, clearly enough. But who are you? It's no use saying you know who you are just because you tell me you can fit your particular key into a particular slot, which will only receive your particular key because that's not foolproof and certainly not conclusive.... Occasionally I believe I perceive a little of what you

[5] Methuen, 1968. First broadcast 1960; first performed on the stage 1963.

are but that's pure accident. . . . It's nothing like an accident, it's deliberate, it's a joint pretence. We depend on these accidents, on these contrived accidents, to continue. . . . What you are, or appear to be to me, or appear to be to you, changes so quickly, so horrifyingly, I certainly can't keep up with it and I'm damn sure you can't either. But who you are I can't even begin to recognise, and sometimes I recognise it so wholly, so forcibly, I can't look, and how can I be certain of what I see? You have no number. Where am I to look, where am I to look, what is there to locate so as to have some surety? . . . You're the sum of so many reflections. How many reflections? Whose reflections? Is that what you consist of?

This long discussion in which Pinter precisely notes our flashes of awareness of people and our sudden sense that we do not know them at all, is the climax of a scene in which the speaker has already asked, 'What do you do when you're tired, go to bed? . . . What do you do when you wake up? . . . What do you do in the day when you're not walking about? . . . Where do you find a resting place? . . . Why haven't I got a home? . . . Do you believe in God?' and finally, 'Do you know what the point is . . . the point is, who are you?'

In every play, Pinter sets himself to examine just that question, exploring through a character's claim on life and reactions to people what his sense of himself is. Because he is reflecting people as he sees them in the mid-century, the figures who emerge are shadowy, tenuous, menaced, groping after an identity they cannot maintain, hiding behind a role which is false, shifting their ground in relation to each other in order to pursue their own advantage; yet claiming our pity and involvement with them because their search is for themselves. Because Pinter expresses so many of the ideas, fragmentarily or in detail, that we have glanced at in the last few pages, and because he is a writer of drama, and therefore, as I suggested earlier, by the very form of his writing begs the question of identity most urgently, it is of value to look at one of his plays, *The Caretaker*,[6] in detail.

This play was first produced in 1960 and revolves round three characters, Davies, Aston and Mick. Aston gives Davies shelter

[6] Methuen, 1960.

when he has no job, home or money. He shares with him the room he lives in, one full of old junk at the top of an otherwise empty house owned by his brother Mick. Aston gives Davies tobacco, a bed, shoes, clothes, and offers him a job as caretaker. Davies, who goes under the assumed name of Jenkins, wants to collect his 'papers' from Sidcup which prove who he really is. But the weather is bad and his shoes unsuitable. Mick, Aston's brother, treats Davies unpredictably, sometimes contemptuously mocking him, sometimes asking his advice and help. Unexpectedly, after Aston has offered Davies the job as caretaker, Mick does too.

When Davies becomes convinced that Mick is the owner of the house (he 'has the deeds'—compare Davies's 'papers'), he tries to play the brothers off against each other to his own advantage. Aston confides in him about his stay in a mental hospital and Davies always afterwards regards him as 'nutty'. He attempts to take his place in the house, ejecting him. But Aston orders him out, and when he seeks redress from Mick, the latter turns on him, accusing him of lying about his professional qualifications and insulting his brother. He orders him to go. Davies turns back to Aston, but he has no hope there. Movingly, the play ends with the rejected and, in one way, self-ejected caretaker again out of a job, with no point to his life, no home, no money and no name. Perhaps if he could get his papers? . . .

And what is the play *about* as compared to what is its plot? John Russell Taylor quotes a puzzled interlocutor, inquiring of the author, 'But what are your plays *about*, Mr Pinter?' and receiving the answer, 'The weasel under the cocktail cabinet.'[7] The menace, that is, that lies ready to pounce hidden beneath the veneer of the civilized world we move about in. If this is what Pinter's plays are about generally, *The Caretaker* specifically, I think, would be fairly interpreted as the old pattern of *Paradise Lost*. Some people have argued that it is about a man whose deep relationship with his brother is threatened by the new friendship that the brother has made, and who deliberately engineers the downfall of that friendship so that he can have his brother all to himself again. There

7 John Russell Taylor, *Anger and After* (Penguin, 1963).

is this element in it, but I do not think it is the whole play, or even its main emphasis.

At the play's centre is the shifty figure of Davies himself, Everyman of the 1960s, finding a paradise and losing it. Vague about his origins, indeterminate about his race, doubtful about his personal history, though with vivid circumstantial accounts of isolated incidents, he boasts, 'I can always turn my hand to most things . . . Give me . . ., give me a bit of time to pick it up.' He is an odd-job man. His main characteristics are suspicion, a certain shifty cunning in acquisitiveness, and a lostness with which he begins and ends the play, which shows all too clearly when he tries to manipulate events: 'You get a bit out of your depth sometimes, don't you?' says Mick. His suspicion is of anything in the material world whose workings he does not understand—the electric fire, the gas oven. Or of any peoples or races who seem alien, who take the house next door or usurp Englishmen's jobs in the cafeteria. Or, finally, of anyone whose motives he cannot enter into. Mick shows him hostility to begin with. He can begin to understand Mick. But Aston has shown him only kindness, kindness with no obvious self-advantage in it. So he cannot understand Aston and is quick to associate it with Aston's abnormality, as shown in the way he collects junk, his inability to get on with the job, and his stay in a mental home.

His grasping at advantage emerges in the whole pattern of the play as he attempts to play off the brothers against each other, and it appears also in his begging more money from Aston before he has had a chance to spend the first lot he has been given, his seizing of the bag of clothes, knowing it is not his, and so on. More subtly, it lies in the gradual change in his tone from grateful appreciation to a bullying demand for his rights—'rights' is one of his key words—culminating in his attempts to turn Aston out of his own room.

But more fundamental than any of this in Davies's character is the fact that he is lost. He enters the scene having lost his job: his 'papers' have been in Sidcup for—vaguely—about fifteen years. So he has lost his identity too. Is he Welsh? He is not sure. 'Well, I've been around, you know . . . what I mean . . . I've been about . . .' Nor where he was born, since 'it's a bit hard, like, to set your mind back'. He has lost his wife, leaving her after a fortnight of marriage. And he has no home and does not know what rest and tranquillity are: 'Sit down? Huh . . . I haven't had a good sit down . . . I haven't had a proper sit down . . . Well, I couldn't tell you.'

So this is Pinter's picture of mid-century man, caretaking the world, lost, suspicious and desperate, holding on to what he can get. But he has his dreams. For Davies it is in finding those papers which will prove everything, for Aston it is in building the shed, creating something, for Mick it is the glamour penthouse of the glossy magazine, 'teal blue, copper and parchment linoleum squares'. And he has his moments of confession, of honest anguish: Davies telling of his treatment in his job, Mick exploding with disappointment that his plans for his brother's care of the house come to so little, and Aston, telling movingly of a sick mind at the mercy of the society which put him away:

> I thought . . . they understood what I said. I mean I used to talk to them. I talked too much. That was my mistake. . . . Anyway, someone must have said something. . . . And some kind of lie must have got around. Then one day they took me to hospital. . . . I didn't want to go.

When, after shock treatment, he is released,

> The trouble was . . . my thoughts . . . had become very slow. . . . I couldn't think at all . . . I couldn't hear what people were saying. . . . And I laid everything out, in order, in my room, all the things I knew were mine, but I didn't die. The thing is, I should have been dead. I should have died. Anyway I feel much better now. But I don't talk to people now.

Yet Aston, in a deep sense, is healthy. Far stronger even than his urge to revenge himself on those who had done this to him, is his desire to create:

> I've often thought of going back and trying to find the man who did that to me. But I want to do something first. I want to build that shed out in the garden.

Their relationships are shifty, uncertain. Davies is at first bewildered and then aggressive. Mick dances round Davies mentally, delivering knock-out blows whenever he feels inclined. And Aston's first attempt to build a relationship after the isolation following his mental illness is doomed to failure because he cannot reach Davies as a person, and does not try. After his long confession he no longer talks to him, because the confessional need has gone, because he cannot bear his noise and his smell, cannot endure him as he is; and this communicates itself to Davies. 'Waking an old man up in the middle of the night, you must be off your nut! . . . What do you want me to do, stop breathing?' he grumbles, when Aston tries to stop his disturbing noise during the night. 'Why do you invite me in here in the first place?' he asks. Why indeed? *Was* it kindness, or was Aston fulfilling his own need just as much, though more subtly, than Mick and Davies?

One could go on in this play to show how it points the modern clinging to material facts—the junk, the shed, the house, the desire for a clock to tell the time, the topographical and biographical details with which Mick bewilderingly refers to his relatives. (The desire for verification, Pinter said, is understandable but cannot always be satisfied. 'There are no hard distinctions between what is real and what is unreal.') Or we might note the growing sense of insecurity and menace or the absurdly (in the full sense) funny situations and dialogue which arise. But there is no space to dwell further on all these.

Popular reaction to Pinter has been very mixed. He hits off perhaps too clearly one view of today's world:

> I wouldn't mind if there were a hinter
> Joy or beauty or even a glinter
> Light or vision or promise. The stinter!
> Well, I mean, he doesn't beginter
> Look for 'vases' (or spring in winter)
> His desolate desert is almost skinter
> Everything we might say is akinter
> Humanity, like looking inter
> The last dry cactus. In fact it's a sin ter
> Destroy so utterly, and to splinter
> The bare bones to the sun, like Pinter.

The reaction of this poem[8] (written by a student on first reading Pinter's *The Birthday Party*) is that there is more to life than Pinter allows, that relationships are not universally aggressive, menacing and self-seeking (even if they often are), but that our sense of chaos is the more vivid because we are contrasting it with an imaginable harmony and order.

We are moved by Pinter's foolish and lost Caretaker as we are moved by Beckett's bewildered and pathetic, and yet alive, tramps, because in them we recognize a human condition, in them we see ourselves. But this is not the full story of the human condition; there is a chapter left out and the chapter is still to be told. Pinter and Beckett describe with complete honesty man without God. But this is not all there is to be said about man. Ruth Pitter has sounded the other note in her poem, 'Help, Good Shepherd':

> . . . still
> Sound with thy crook the darkling flood,
> Still range the sides of shelvy hill
> And call about in underwood:
>
> For on the hill are many strayed,
> Some held in thickets plunge and cry,
> And the deep waters make us afraid,
> Come then and help us, or we die.[9]

It is a cry which Christians know has been answered; and is answered; and will be answered. In the next chapter we shall look at something of what that answer involves.

[8] 'Too kind to Harold', published in *The Collegian*, Chester, 1968.
[9] From 'Help, Good Shepherd', *Urania* (Cresset Press, 1951).

7 'UNAFRAID TO BE'
The Christian affirmation

Always, wherever, whatever, however,
When I am able to resist
For once the constant pressure of failure to exist,
Let me remember
That truly to be man is to be *man aware of Thee*
And unafraid to be. So help me God.[1]

We must be quite clear on this. The Christian is a man. He does not suddenly take on an angelic nature (in the proper sense of the phrase) when he accepts Christ's Lordship. 'Be an angel' is an exhortation none of us can ever begin to obey—nor, I think, should any of us wish to. We should be denying the exciting and unique role that God has planned for us, created us for, if we did. Truly to be a Christian, therefore, is to be truly man, man as he was meant to be, created to be.

This means that the Christian understands his being in the same kinds of context as other men. When he examines who and what he is, when he ponders over the 'nature of man', he is compelled to define it in just the same terms as everyone else, in terms of relationships, task, values and location. And he defines it in the context of the same problems. That is, he too has to encounter the same shifting uncertainties of relationships; he has to face within himself and in the world in which he stands the great blank question of meaninglessness; he has to examine the reasonableness of his own

[1] From David Gascoyne, 'Fragments towards a *religio poetae*', *op. cit.* (my italics).

activity—his job, what he spends his time doing; and he has to find his own relation to home, the place where he lives, the spot where his roots go down.

But he understands these in a different way; he has a different perspective from that of man-without-God, or man-with-any-other-god. It is not merely that his life in God provides a yardstick which makes non-Christian values seem not so much false as irrelevant, but that every medium by which the Christian locates who and what he is, is charged with, shot through by, the God he serves. *All* relationships, personal and social, with Christian and non-Christian, are based for him on God's relationship with man; all his values necessarily are in Christian terms; his sense of task or vocation is not just partly but wholly determined by his sense of being completely in God's hands; his sense of time and place is conditioned by his awareness of God at work in *this* moment, in *that* precise topographical spot.

THE HABIT OF LOVING

We must begin, where God began for us, with relationships. We saw in the last chapter how much this was the concern of contemporary writers, and how uncertainty in one's encounters with people, knowing the shifts and changes of personalities, was linked very strongly with lack of certainty about oneself. We saw, too, how this connected with uncertainty about everything, so that doubts rose about whether 'anything meant anything at all', whether there were any meaning to be attributed to life. It is quite impossible to separate these, and in fact the New Testament in its assertion of what life is about directly links together relationships and a meaning in life. Christ's recorded statement 'I am come that you might have life, and have it more abundantly' is linked with the statement His actual pattern of living made, and what His obedience to death said, and what His empty tomb declared.

If, that is, the answer to meaninglessness is to be found in the Christian faith, it is to be found in what Jesus had to say, by word and deed and dying and living, about the relationship between God and man and that resulting from it between man and man.

There is an incident recorded where this was made quite explicit.[2] A lawyer stood up and tested him saying 'Teacher, what shall I do to inherit eternal life?' Eternal life in any human context, two thousand years ago or today, means basically, How can this 'I' go on being, avoid being blotted out? It does not mean, of course, simply existing continuously and incessantly; Swift has made horrifyingly vivid, in *Gulliver's Travels*, Voyage III in the encounter with the Struldbrugs, what 'eternal life' means if thought of merely quantitively instead of qualitatively. We shall look at this point in greater detail later. When the lawyer demanded his question of Jesus, though, in the context of his day and cult, it would mean, How can this 'I' survive not only death but judgment? For today's man, the question seems different. Nothingness is the sting, not judgment. He is questioning survival of any kind after death, not the judgment to be met in it.[3] Yet the question is fundamentally the same: How can I go on, in spite of any barriers my own age perceives, being this unique individual 'me' as the worlds spin and the centuries pass? How can the 'me' inside 'me' stay 'me' for ever and ever?

> All we can pray is
>   Save us from nothingness.
> Nonentity, the universal dread,
> Which makes us feel an irrational pity for the dead,
> And fight the anodyne
> Even while we long for deliverance from pain.[4]

Of course, there will be special emphasis for the questioner and the hearers in every generation of men. But basically, that was what the question meant and what it means for us all today too, whether we are living in digs in Birmingham, or raising a young family in

[2] Luke 10:25–28.

[3] To put this another way, the only 'judgment' which holds any meaning for today's man is the condemnation to chaos in this life and nothingness after it.

[4] From Anne Ridler, 'A Matter of Life and Death' in *A Matter of Life and Death* (Faber and Faber, 1959).

a 'semi', or arguing logical positivism over a brew of black coffee in a smoky study-bedroom. What shall I do to inherit eternal life? What is the secret of true and perpetual identity?

The reply Christ drew (from the questioner himself) was a brief but profound summary of the law of life as the Jewish people had received and understood it. 'You shall love the Lord your God with all your heart, and with all your soul, and with all your strength, and with all your mind; and your neighbour as yourself.' So the secret of an identity that *means* something is in some way connected with relationships that *mean* something. 'Do this, and you will live' was the pungent summary.

THE ULTIMATE IN NEIGHBOURS

Volumes have been and will be written on the implications of this. At this point we can only glance at one or two ideas connected with it. There has been in the last few decades much writing and thinking about the link between the love of God and the love of man. For many people they are synonymous: in view of the pre-occupations of earlier chapters of this book we need to concentrate on this connection here. It is quite true that they *are* generically related. But we need to put them into proper sequence. Loving man does not inevitably indicate loving God: but loving God should, if entered into fully and sacrificially and joyfully, inevitably involve loving man.

And we need to take this a stage further. We should not know how to love either man or God if in the first place we had not learnt the habit of loving from Him. To put it quite simply: I love man because I love God, and I love God because in the first place He loves me. That is ultimately what the whole of the Bible is about; that is what the message of the living Christian church today in the twentieth century is about. Man *can* love man because he *can* love God, because God *does* love him. And this, of course, is where the meaning comes into life. We can understand our own act of loving God only in terms of His act in loving us; and all other relationships, the ones stressed by present-day writers, find their bases in this.

This was the point of the story Jesus told to clarify and emphasize the truth to which His questioner had paid lip service. The 'story of the Good Samaritan' was in reply to the lawyer's question. 'And who is my neighbour?' is a most relevant question for us today as we look not only at national, ideological and racial barriers but at group barriers also—the Us and Them habit of mind which is so subtle and persistent a temptation, whether we see ourselves in the vanguard of progress or as defenders of rightful traditions. In the story it is the Good Samaritan who is the 'neighbour': and yet the parable arose from the challenge to love other people—'neighbours'—as one does oneself. So what we have is a story showing someone actually doing the loving, living out the relationship, to illustrate who and what a neighbour is and what creates neighbourly love. For part of the rich meaning of that parable is that one creates 'neighbours' by being one; *it is a relationship which can be established by one person at one end of it*. So when I am commanded to 'love my neighbour as myself', I find a neighbour as soon as I act as a neighbour, *am* a neighbour to someone. By definition he then becomes a neighbour to me whether he has chosen to or not.

The story of the Good Samaritan was told to illustrate the law of eternal life, which was to 'love God' with all that one has, and one's fellow as oneself. And for us, with hindsight, spectators of a cross towards which the man who told the story was travelling, there is an extra depth in the story. For Christ's own presence at that moment among His fellow-men was a direct affirmation that God, too, acted as neighbour, *was* neighbour to man. And by being, by His presence there in our midst, our neighbour, He made *us* neighbours to Himself, with the same obligation of love and concern; with the same delight in His existence. By making Himself neighbour to us He risked bearing the kind of neighbours we would choose to be to Him.

I am not moved to love thee, my Lord God,
by the Heaven thou hast promised me:
I am not moved by the sore dreaded hell
to forbear me from offending thee.

I am moved by thee, Lord; I am moved
at seeing thee nailed upon the cross and mocked:
I am moved by thy body all over wounds:

I am moved by thy dishonour and thy death.

I am moved, last, by thy love, in such a wise
that though there were no heaven I still should love thee,
and though there were no hell I still should fear thee.

I need no gift of thee to make me love thee;
For though my present hope were all despair,
As now I love thee I should love thee still.[5]

WHAT IS IT LIKE?

Our ability to respond, then, to love God in the all-in way that
is the response of our whole selves, is the result of God's love for *us*,
something He stirs and stimulates within us. 'We love him,' John
writes, 'because he first loved us.' So *our* love is shaped, defined, given
its distinctive quality, by His. And in this loving of God and of each
other we find who and what we really are. It is obviously relevant,
therefore, to ask what kind of love this is which is shaping ours.
What is His love like? Clearly this, too, is a subject for volumes.[6]

Of the many things that should be said here about 'what this
love is like', there are two that seem to stand out as being specially
relevant for today as we have seen it outlined earlier. One is the
sheer dynamic creativity of this love; the other is its sacrificial nature.

The Christian belief is that man is God's creature, created
originally to be like Him. ('Let us', the creation account in Genesis
reads, 'make man in our image, after our likeness.') But, and this is
the all-important point for twentieth-century man, the anti-hero,
this is a love which does not rejoice only in what it has made, but
loves even when the making is marred. It is a love which not only
creates but re-creates, amends and empowers. So it is dynamically
effective and to be enjoyed even when man is despairing of himself,
aware of the 'end of innocence' and the darkness of his heart. John
put it in this way: 'We are God's children now; it does not yet
appear what we shall be, but we know that when he appears we
shall be like him.'[7] So it is a love which goes on creating, goes

[5] Miguel de Guavera, 'Sonnet', trans. Samuel Beckett, from *An
Anthology of Mexican Poetry* (Thames and Hudson, 1959).

[6] John 21:25.   [7] 1 John 3:2.

on shaping, goes on 'picking up the bits'; a love which loves men as they are, not as they would like to be; and by its power it can re-make them.

And it is a sacrificial love. In a sense this is inevitable if it is creative, since making something and caring about it involves by definition being open to the pain of its being spoilt or misused or misunderstood. Again, the Christian understanding of this aspect of God's love comes through its demonstration by Christ. He 'acted out' this loving to the ultimate in pain, this being willing to bear the burden of being involved, right through to the bitter end and beyond. And because this is the kind of love we receive from God, it is the kind of love we learn, slowly, to give; a love that is both creative and sacrificial, our love, shaped by His.

In his letter to the Romans, Paul writes, 'God's love floods our hearts through the Holy Spirit which has been given to us.' And our deepest experience of God's love for us, as Paul urges in this same Epistle, is in our encounter with Christ's sacrifice for us: 'For when we were still in weakness, Christ died in due time for the ungodly. . . . God proves his love for us by this.'[8] Professor C. H. Dodd comments,

> We know divine love experimentally . . . when it becomes a motive in our own hearts, when we, in our measure, love with the love of God. In His perfect measure, Christ loved with the love of God; indeed it is because divine love became incarnate in Him that it *floods our hearts*.

To put this very simply: we cannot avoid the love of God because it extends to each of us, His creatures. We can choose *not* to respond to it; in which case we can attempt to love in our human fashion, and the results of this we looked at in Chapter 6. Alternatively, we can respond to His love; and if we do we can let Him teach us more and more of what loving with the love of God means. One thing is quite certain. If we *do* accept the challenge to let Him teach us about loving, we are leaving ourselves open perpetually to change

---

[8] Romans 5:5-8, based on *The New Translation* by Professor James Moffatt, used by Professor Dodd in his commentary, *The Epistle of Paul to the Romans* (Hodder and Stoughton, 1932; Fontana, 1960).

and growth. For these are the inevitable accompaniments of vitality
—life—eternal life.

WHAT DOES IT DO TO ME?

These factors of change and growth which are part of the vitality
of loving with God's love are very important for us today in view
of two widely prevalent fears. One dark doubt is that to become
a Christian, to love God with all one has, involves losing one's
precious individual identity to take on a stereotype; and the other
is that to become a Christian, to submit oneself to the Lordship
of Christ once and for all, means that one is fixed and has no more
to learn, no further change or development to make; that one is
stuck with it. Yet both these ideas are a denial of the identity God
has given us; both of them derive from a misunderstanding of what
God created us to be.

To begin with, our individual identity is based on our sharing
the nature of all men as God's children, made in His image; when
we respond to His love we share His nature as His adopted sons.
The family characteristic of the Godhead is *vitality*—life.[9] It can
therefore be no part of God's plan for men in general, or any
individual man in particular, to lose this unique vitality, to become
a zombie, a robot, an automaton.

This is what the resurrection is all about. It is the final affirmation
of this sheer, unquenchable life. If we experience most deeply the
kind of love available for us (both to have and to give) in the death
of Jesus, we certainly discover the quality of vitality which is
naturally ours in Christ's rising again. For His literal triumph over
death was, and is, an acting out of this nature, this unquenchable
vitality which is the Father's, and the Son's, and ours—'since thou
hast given him power over all flesh, to give eternal life to all whom
thou hast given him'.[1] When Jesus raised Lazarus from the dead
He was, in John's patterning of the gospel, enacting beforehand
His own encounter with death and His triumph over it. And there
is tremendous poetic power in the way John parallels the two

[9] 'As the Father has life in himself, so he has granted the Son also to
have life in himself' (John 5:26).

[1] John 17:2.

events. But this is not just a 'poetic' truth to be seized on only by our imagination. 'Poet' literally means 'maker', and the profoundly challenging thing about all this is that God is a Poet who writes poems about the inner truth of existence, and then literally brings them to life, 'acts them out' in terms of everyday realities. So it is not just a theoretical 'life principle' overcoming the force of death. It is a real Person going through it dynamically and demonstrating that we, too, may do the same. Thus we may share, if we choose, this family characteristic of vitality.

THE SELF ONE WAS MEANT TO BE

Yet one of the most repeated of Christ's sayings is that concerning being prepared to lose one's life in order to save it. 'Whoever would save his life will lose it; and whoever loses his life for my sake, he will save it.'[2] And attempting to save one's life is in some way connected with the man who 'loses or forfeits himself'. Being prepared to lose it, therefore, for the sake of Christ, somehow means safeguarding, winning, one's *self*. The saying appears in all the Gospels, with a characteristic emphasis in John: 'He who loves his life loses it, and he who hates his life in this world will keep it for eternal life.'[3]

It is easy (and rather dangerous) to be vaguely mystical about this. There is, in accepting Christ, a necessary loss of identity in one sense, in that there has to be a willingness to abdicate from self-control, a shift of focus so that things are not measured by their advantage to *self*. This was glimpsed by those writers we looked at in Chapter 5, who saw man's identity as being found in something objective, something inside himself with which he identifies himself. There is a real truth enshrined in 'The Countess Kathleen',[4] that one must be willing to give up one's soul. (But not to the devil! To the One who has first claim.) But, and this is an important 'but', this does not mean that one ceases to be an individual; it is *not* a movement towards 'mystical incorporation into the divine'. It contradicts the Hindu notion completely. On the contrary, becoming a Christian means *becoming more uniquely the*

[2] Luke 9:24.   [3] John 12:25.
[4] In W. B. Yeats, *Collected Plays* (Macmillan, 1952).

self one was intended to be than ever one could before; means escaping
from the narrow limitations of one's psychological horizons to the
freedom of being God's child.[5]

As W. B. Yeats said,

> Only God my dear,
> Could love you for yourself alone
> And not for your yellow hair.[6]

Yeats's intention in the poem was not to stress God's love, but man's.
In fact, however, the attention he calls to the nature of God's love here
is important. It is 'for one's self alone', what each of us—externals
apart—uniquely is. That is part of the meaning, for instance,
behind Paul's insistence on mutual respect among Christians, when
he was writing to the Romans on controversial matters of opinion.
Of each controversialist Paul says ' . . . God has welcomed him . . .
And he will be upheld, for the Master is able to make him stand.'[7]

But this unique 'him', this individual who will be more truly
himself than ever when he has handed over his innermost self to
Christ, is not a static being: he is not playing a kind of spiritual
'statues', caught in a fixed attitude which will never develop or
change. 'Our knowledge is imperfect . . .', says Paul; 'but when
the perfect comes, the imperfect will pass away.'[8] And therefore
the challenge is to 'grow up in every way into him'. Brunner
writes, 'The knight has been dubbed "knight", but he is still in his
condition a commoner. His nobility has not yet permeated his
whole nature.'[9] And Paul, like Luke quoting the lawyer, quoting
the law, sees this growth as possible through love, the love of God.

> . . . that you, being rooted and grounded in love, may have power
> to comprehend with all the saints what is the breadth and length

---

[5] 'Myself!' writes L. P. Hartley in *The Hireling*. 'It was like saying my
prison, my torture chamber almost . . . something I was condemned
to stay in and never should get out of.'

[6] From 'For Anne Gregory', *Collected Poems* (Macmillan, 1952).

[7] Romans 14:3, 4.

[8] I Corinthians 13:9, 10.

[9] In *Man in Revolt* (1942), quoted by Michael Green in *The Meaning
of Salvation* (Hodder and Stoughton, 1965).

and height and depth, and to know the love of Christ which surpasses knowledge, that you may be filled with all the fullness of God.[1]

This is something in the Christian faith to which we must pay particular attention. Becoming a Christian means beginning a long journey, God-directed all the way, until we develop into the beings we shall by grace one day become. Too often we limit the truth and power of God to what we have already experienced, instead of being open and ready to what He is going to teach us, often through the most unexpected people and in the most unlikely circumstances. Finding our proper Christian identity involves a process of growth comparable to that of the baby; and we shall never fully discover ourselves, if through pride or sloth we allow ourselves to become spiritually retarded.

So the kind of love with which God loves us, with which He teaches us to respond, through which He endows us with identity, is one personal and sensitive enough to meet us each as individuals, and big enough to stimulate and contain growth beyond our wildest imaginings. It is a love which both recognizes *me* and yet dominates me:

> This Man looks like all that I ask of God—
> I can call him both me and master.[2]

And because of this, our love of God which is the special, personal, individual sacrifice that only each individual can make; which is growing and developing all the time: this love has the fundamental quality of obedience. Again, this quality is shaped in our loving by what He Himself has taught us. He taught us how to love obediently by doing it Himself. The great hymn in the Epistle to the Philippians sums it up:

> Have this mind among yourselves, which you have in Christ Jesus, . . . Being found in human form he humbled himself and became obedient unto death, even death on a cross. Therefore God has highly exalted him and bestowed on him the name which is

[1] Ephesians 3:17-19.
[2] From James Brabazon, 'The Face on the Turin Shroud', *Modern Religious Verse* (Studio Vista, 1966).

above every name, that at the name of Jesus every knee should bow . . .[3]

Who are we, what are we? God's children, unique, individual, taught to love Him, stimulated to grow, challenged to obedience. And all these factors in our identity interest and affect each other. Charles Williams has a splendid poem[4] on the parable of the wedding garment, in which the 'wedding garment' insisted on is a test of obedience in much the same sense that the apple is in the second and third chapters of Genesis. The footman has to bar the door to all not wearing it:

> Sir, tonight
> is strictly kept as strictly given;
> . . . all require
> virtues and beauty not their own
> e'er genuflecting at the Throne . . .
> This guest his brother's carriage wore;
> that, his wife's zeal, while just before,
> she in his steady patience shone;
> there a young lover had put on
> the fine integrity of sense
> his mistress used; . . .
> No he or she was he or she
> merely: no single being dared,
> except the Angels of the Guard,
> come without other kind of dress
> than his poor life had to profess . . .
> into another's glory given,
> bright ambiguities of Heaven.

The point Charles Williams is making is that the quality of obedience in our love, which He has taught us and stirred up in us, blossoms into new virtues and powers in the growing person who is the Christian. And this shows itself in our relationship with our fellow beings.

---

[3] Philippians 2:5–10.
[4] 'Apologue on the Parable of the Wedding Garment', *Time and Tide*.

'Love your neighbour as yourself', quoted the lawyer. 'The commandments . . . are summed up in this sentence, "You shall love your neighbour as yourself"', commented Paul.[5]

'Love' is God's supreme commandment to men. Love is an objective value, rooted in God; it is no passing emotion, changing as our feelings change. It is *the* value of mankind. And it is a value which we can understand and live by because God has loved us and thereby made it possible for us truly to love others.

This is the proper basis, as the Christian sees it, of that respect for the human being simply because he is a human being, which we saw in earlier chapters as being the one value that modern writers accepted. It is, too, the basis of that responsibility, that 'being members one of another' which we noted in the last chapter. A respect for, a concern for, a responsibility for other people, because they also are made in the image of God, are also the object of His love, is obviously going to affect our own behaviour to them in the context of family, friends, acquaintances and society generally.

This leads us on to notice the extraordinary balance there is between human and spiritual awareness in our entering into and developing of human relationships. It is a twofold process. On the one hand God's love for us and ours for Him informs the possible depth and vitality of all our human relationships. This is not always, of course, a conscious thing. We do not necessarily spend our time with someone we love thinking 'God is in me loving this person'; it is simply that God informs, vitalizes that involvement we have with the other. At the same time, while we are learning more of the one we love because of God at work within us, we are also learning more of the God we love because of the active encounter with another human being. Within the terms and outworkings of human relationships we learn more of our own individual relationship with God and that of 'man' in general. So the forces are kept in continuous tension: more of God through man; more of man through God; more of one's self through the whole complex of relationships this involves.

As an offshoot of this, those virtues which we do not easily covet, which are no part of our temperamental desire, become the

5 Romans 13:9.

object of our respect when they are demonstrated by people whom we have learnt to honour as fellow-creatures of God; and a respect for them is a movement towards a growth into them:

> . . . magnificence
> a father borrowed of his son,
> who was not there ashamed to don
> his father's wise economy.[6]

It is not an original thought, but it bears repetition, that there is great danger for the Christian in type-casting himself, in saying, 'I can't ever be like that: I'm not that kind of person.' The exciting thing about Christian identity is that there are no limits to the kind of person God can shape us into being. And when we love our neighbours as profoundly as we love ourselves, He is using this, too, to do the shaping.

WHAT'S HIS JOB?

One of the ways in which we can better understand and work out our relationship with God and our fellows is in the practice of the task given to us. You will remember that this was one of the questions Arthur Miller saw as helping to define a character entering a play: 'How does he live, make a living?' 'What does he *do*?' is the way we put it usually. So let's put the question. What, in the Christian view, does man *do*? How does he live, make a living?

'THE WORK DONE TO KEEP ME ALIVE, TO DO THE WORK FOR WHICH I LIVE'

It is a question that has to be answered on two levels, and keeping them in proper tension with each other is one of the problems that beset us all. On the one hand man's task is to make a living in the kind of world in which he finds himself, whatever its social/economic pattern. On the other, he recognizes that his fundamental task, that given to man by God, is to exercise dominion over nature, to fill the earth and subdue it, and to enjoy 'acceptance' with God.[7] In some generations and some civilizations, including

[6] Charles Williams, *op. cit.*   [7] See God's words to Cain in Genesis 4:7.

the one described in some books of the Old Testament, there was no sharp dichotomy between the two. But one of the great problems for the Christian in a modern, industrial, capitalist society (or communist either, for that matter) is the working out in terms of daily life of the task given him by God. The conditions of work seem so completely at variance with the divine ordinances of duty.

This problem of 'the meaning of work' and 'Christian vocation' in a highly sophisticated and material society has been analysed elsewhere at length and needs no detailed study here.[8] The main point, of course, that makes God's task for man, as biblically recorded, seem irrelevant for us today, is the dichotomy between work and life. 'Work' is not merely distanced from the natural rhythm of things, but seems to have no rhythm at all, seems pointless and of no intrinsic value. Therefore the only point to work becomes the money; there seems little joy or dedication in the work itself. Hence the pressure in today's society (and however deep our Christian commitment this pressure is a fierce one) to evaluate any task in the terms of the wages or salary apportioned to it. It is an almost inevitable reaction when one's job seems to be so irrelevant to 'subduing' or 'exercising dominion' over nature in any sense. In spite, therefore, of automation and the present attempts to give us all a wider understanding of the relevance of our labour, our ideas of work have, as a society, been conditioned by what we have known, and by our daily experience; often a meaningless monotony. One's *real* living, therefore, comes in one's interests apart from work:

> . . . How I fail
> daily to make sense of a sense of loss!
> . . . This bridge is a landmark
> dividing my day: the work done to keep
> me alive, to do the work for which I live . . .
> . . . I survive
> merely a day's weariness, the weather's mood . . .
> . . . I go and come, arrive

[8] See A. R. Osborn, *Christian Ethics* (OUP, 1940), and, for a more detailed and up-to-date work, H. F. R. Catherwood, *The Christian Citizen* (Hodder and Stoughton, 1969).

home as a dog to his master, the ball
of the spent day sticking in my throat. I
go and come at dayrise and at nightfall
to the same place and at the same time by
the same bus, I go and come, yet always
seem to be here where the traffic slows down . . .[9]

And so work is valueless for the living awareness of the individual, except in terms of the material gains it brings. Living in conditions like this, how can we, therefore, hold in proper tension our routine, perhaps 'soul-destroying', job on the one hand and what we have understood to be God's job for man on the other?

'EXERCISING DOMINION'

There are obviously no easy answers. But I think we need to consider more deeply what 'exercising dominion over nature' really means before we groan too loudly about the irrelevance of the Genesis command to man in the twentieth century. Obviously, every break-through in industry, engineering and the sciences is an obedience to this original command; every space flight, every surgical operation, even transplanting organs, has a relevance to it. The ethical problems associated with them should be thought out, surely, in relation to it. So, just as the Victorians saw their 1851 Great Exhibition, which rejoiced in industry, in a religious context, as demonstrating how man, under God, could control and over-come natural forces, it should be possible to consider all scientific developments in the same context. But the tragedy is that man no longer sees his dominion over the world as under God, and his 'subduing' of the earth is to his own glory, not his Lord's.

All these advances are part of the activity of man as a species. But most of us as individuals have not much to do with either space flights or transplant surgery or any other such obvious conquests of nature. Yet the command is an individual as well as a racial one. How, then?

One way of 'exercising dominion' over nature—of entering into

[9] From Zulfikar Ghose, 'Kew Bridge', *Jets from Orange* (Macmillan, 1967).

our possession of it—which we too often forget is simply and thankfully rejoicing in it. The beauties of nature in which we take joy have in a sense become our possession, given to us by that Lord who gave us 'richly all things to enjoy'. We have much to learn as Christians from writers like Dylan Thomas and Laurie Lee who have understood this:

If ever I saw blessing in the air
   I see it now in this still early day
Where lemon-green the vaporous morning drips
   Wet sunlight on the powder of my eye.

Blown bubble-film of blue, the sky wraps round
   Weeds of warm light whose every root and rod
Splutters with soapy green. And all the world
   Sweats with the bead of summer in its bud.

If ever I heard blessing it is there
   Where birds in trees that shoals and shadows are
Splash with their hidden wings and drops of sound
   Break on my ears their crests of throbbing air.

Pure in the haze the emerald sun dilates,
   The lips of sparrow milk the mossy stones,
While white as water by the lake a girl
   Swims her green hand among the gathered swans.

Now, as the almond burns its smoking wick,
   Dropping small flames to light the candled grass;
Now, as my low blood scales its second chance,
   If ever world were blessed, now it is.[1]

Yet another element in the task given man was to 'be fruitful, multiply, and fill the earth . . .' For the tribal society, being fruitful, having expanding families, was obviously as effective a way of subduing the earth as any. But for us today there is still a funda-mental relevance in the command, for behind it is the vision of an orderly and harmonious social structure based on a pattern of family

[1] Laurie Lee, 'April Rise', *The Bloom of Candles* (John Lehmann, 1947).

life which involved authority, loyalty, obedience and trust. So it calls into question our whole concept of the family unit in today's society, its harmony and orderliness, and its basic importance; and here again we are brought up against the bedrock, the basis for those values we have seen modern writers asserting. The tie of blood relationship finds its *human* value here: the sense of 'finding oneself' through family relationships, and that family 'finding itself' through its key role in society. All this is involved in the command. For today's Christian, in today's society, the task is even more compelling, simply because today's Christian, in so small a world where his 'flocks' graze over two continents instead of a couple of fields, must often think of 'family' in much wider terms. Who are his 'brothers'? And yet surely the vocation for many Christians will still be to create Christian homes whose families reflect the order and harmony of that first command, whose loyalty and love and obedience are factors in 'subduing the earth' in the terms and methods of the twentieth century.

'DOING WELL'

The key to all this must be the recognition that 'the earth is the Lord's' and that whatever task we do is therefore under Him. The New Testament rephrases the job God has given man to do in quite clear and simple terms:

> Work out your own salvation with fear and trembling; for God is at work in you, both to will and to work for his good pleasure.[2]

If it is a job under God we are doing we have to learn the hard fact that He has the right to reject it if it is not done with integrity. (The marvellous thing is the grace with which He uses our botched-up attempts when they are all we have been able to achieve.) The story of Cain's sacrifice and its rejection is a good illustration of this. When he was attempting sacrifice to God, so the Genesis account runs, he was told, 'If you do well, will you not be accepted?' 'Doing well' in the Old Testament becomes in the New Testament 'working out your own salvation', recognizing one's relationship with God and working out the practical implications of this—

[2] Philippians 2:12, 13.

Give me above the deep intent
The deed, the deed[3]

in daily being and doing. So our task, the job He has given us to do, is, as the old Scottish catechism puts it, 'to glorify God and to enjoy Him for ever', to work out in all we do and are that joyous knowledge of God Himself that being Christians gives us.

Inevitably this will lead us to a re-focusing of our daily tasks. We will find there are some, perhaps, in today's society, that we cannot undertake because they cut across our Christian vocation. Atomic scientists have had to face this problem in some aspects of their work. Doctors in Nazi Germany had similar soul-searching to do, sometimes, when called, for instance, to undertake a social hygiene that involved the extermination of the physically delicate or inadequate in order to purify the race physically. For a Christian the balance, the tension, between God's calling and society's *must* be maintained. Render to Caesar the things that are Caesar's; and to God the things that are God's.

THE RIGHTS AND THE WRONGS

This thinking about our identity has led us from 'Who am I?'—God's child, loved by Him and loving Him, 'What am I?'—God's servant, with a task to fulfil that can be understood and under-taken only in terms of our relationship with God—to 'How do I do it?'

Such questions must challenge us to reassess our values. How do I understand, for instance, 'wrong' and 'right'? Every generation asks these questions in specific terms, relates them to particular situations. What are the 'wrongs' and 'rights' of the war in Vietnam? Or of drug-taking? How far do I go in physical expression of affection and sexual attraction? *And what determines my answers* to all these questions and to many more?

PEOPLE MATTER MORE THAN THINGS

Quite clearly we are once again up against the problem of what 'goes' in today's society balanced against what 'goes' in the

[3] From John Drinkwater, 'A Prayer'.

Christian view of man. We have already seen that the contemporary world is extremely self-critical in some things, and less than honest in others. It recognizes, for instance, that something is wrong with its scale of values when 'people' are sacrificed for 'things', when the only antidote it can offer to a sick soul is an aspirin and a redecoration of the living room:

> The bodily comforts, Sweetie. That's us, isn't it? The great providers—in time of trouble. A roof, a fire—one hot drink, one soft bed—the knife is six inches deep in his soul—and we feed him. Meat and two veg. We help him—'the way to dusty death'—hmmm? We make it easy for him—I mean, that's it—the whole bit—easy—and no fuss. Specially—no fuss![4]

So 'people matter more than things', which is the plea behind this passage, is some sort of a framework, something we can make do with in the western world. But it does not get us all that far, particularly if we are vague about who and what people are. What happens, for instance, when people come up against *people*? Is it all a matter of subjective judgment? Is the man who is sincere, who is completely convinced he is right, thereby justified? If my interests clash with my next-door neighbour's, by what criterion do we decide the rights and wrongs of it? We are both people.

The point is obvious. A vague desire to 'do the decent thing', undefined, with no basis beyond subjective wish and a mind of woolly goodwill, provides no firm ethical structure. Man does not instinctively 'will the good': there is *no* 'needs must' about 'loving the highest when we see it'—(even if we *do* see it, and mostly we do not). Our ethical values, our sense of right and wrong, to have any firmness and stability, must be rooted in something deeper and more substantial, something more objective than our vague well-wishing.

'THE BIT YOU'RE SUPPOSED TO FANCY'

Terry, the character in *Talking to a Stranger* I quoted above, is expecting an illegitimate baby. She is lonely and emotionally desolate. Aware of the inadequacies of the kind of life she is living,

[4] John Hopkins, *Talking to a Stranger*.

the kind of life her home offered, she is *most* deeply aware of her own personal limitations and need. She defines sin for us:

> I didn't know what sin was. Sin! You know? Till it was part of life. I mean, you fancy a bit—and if it isn't the bit you're supposed to fancy! . . .

Finding out what 'you're supposed to fancy' is obviously the thing to do. The New Testament says the same things in different words: 'Look carefully then how you walk, not as unwise men but as wise . . . Understand what the will of the Lord is.'[5] And Terry makes her problem clearer yet:

> I've always thought I'd make a great Christian . . . I've always thought I'd be great with the suffering bit if I knew—really—knew what it was all about.

Ethics, then, the values we apply in any concrete situation, the 'how' of our identity, are the practical working out of our knowing—really—knowing what it is all about. And that involves accepting something beyond our own selfish values: involves accepting the possibility of right and wrong judged not by 'I think' and 'it seems to me', but by 'God's demand', 'God has required'. The prophets of Israel did not say 'we think God would like us to do this'; they cried, 'Thus says the Lord'. And so did Christ. Right and wrong, in any situation, are determined by the obedience of our love for Him; nothing else will do. And that obedience could be achieved only when we 'knew—really—knew what it was all about'.[6]

John Wain has suggested vividly the price we have paid for our self-deluding abandonment of an objective structure of values, in a poem on the dropping of the atomic bomb on Nagasaki:

> Hell is a furnace, so the wise men taught.
> The punishment for sin is to be broiled.
> A glowing coal for every sinful thought.

[5] Ephesians 5:15-17.
[6] On the subject of ethics, see further C. S. Lewis, *The Four Loves* (Geoffrey Bles, 1960); Helen Oppenheimer, *The Character of Christian Morality* (Faith Press, 1965); B. Häring, *The Law of Christ*, trans. E. G. Kaiser (Mercier Press, 1961).

The heat of God's great furnace ate up sin,
Which whispered up in smoke or fell in ash:
So that each hour a new hour could begin. . . .

Hell fried the criminal but burnt the crime,
Purged where it punished, healed where it destroyed:
It was a stove that warmed the rooms of time.

No man begrudged the flames their appetite.
All were afraid of fire, yet none rebelled.
The wise men taught that hell was just and right. . . .

The wise men passed. The clever men appeared.
They ruled that hell be called a pumpkin face.
They robbed the soul of what it justly feared.

Coal after coal the fires of hell went out.
Their heat no longer warmed the rooms of time,
Which glistened now with fluorescent doubt. . . .

Those emblematic flames sank down to rest;
But metaphysical fire can not go out:
Men ran from devils they had dispossessed,

And felt within their skulls the dancing heat . . .

So time dried out and youngest hearts grew old.
The smoky minutes cracked and broke apart.
The world was roasting but the men were cold.

Now from this pain worse pain was brought to birth,
More hate, more anguish, till at last they cried,
'Release this fire to gnaw the crusty earth:

Make it a flame that's obvious to sight
And let us say we kindled it ourselves,
To split the skulls of men and let in light.

Since death is camped among us, wish him joy.

encounter Christ or not, He intervened in human life. I can reject
it or take it within myself, but it does not alter its actuality. My
rejection affects its significance and effectiveness *for me*, but it does
not affect the event. Man after the resurrection is potentially different
from pre-resurrection man. That is what Easter is all about. He
is a different potential identity, for him to enter into or not. One
danger of Existentialism in Christian thinking is that it could, if
held vaguely, identify God with what I can understand of Him
in terms of my own experience, instead of seeing my own
experience as part of the total human experience which is again
infinitesimal part of what is to be known about the divine.

GOD OF THE WHOLE HUMAN FAMILY

...rd Niebuhr also pointed out another danger, this time in
...egaardian Existentialism. He saw it as falsely individualistic,
...ugh all decisions were made *for* ourselves and *by* ourselves
... as *in* ourselves'. Hence he insists that the encounter must be
...tood in a social context. Either in despair or faith, we
...express our understanding simply in terms of 'I'. *We* are
...d, and every 'I' confronts destiny in *our* salvation or dam-
...-what will become of *us*? What is *our* whence and whither?
...od thought that the gospel is not just 'mine'; it is *good news*
...r people. What we are aware of here is something we have
...ntinually right through this study—the tension between
... of corporate man and our personal sense of man the
...l. It reveals itself, for instance, in the New Testament in
...eeping over Jerusalem, in Paul's sense of tragedy because
...ction of Christ by his kinsmen and race. It shows itself
...the modern sense of a *society* sick, rather than merely an
... writer.
...it is here, finally, in our sense of the corporate, that the
...ffirmation of locality can be made. 'As for me and my
...till a contemporary relevance, though in a much wider
...ever Joshua meant it. For while God is Lord of the
...He is God of the whole human family: '. . . I bow my
... the Father, from whom every family in heaven and

Invite him to our table and our games.
We cannot judge, but we can still destroy.'[7]

So the fire released by our 'liberation' from the concept of hell,
John Wain suggests in this poem, becomes the flame of the atomic
bomb dropped on Nagasaki.

THE PRICE TO PAY

The basis of this poem is a profoundly moving analysis of one of
the major moral problems of our time, the dropping of the atomic
bomb. But to it John Wain brings an affirmation of an objective
law of good and evil; and he sees those who deny this law as
releasing upon themselves and the whole world the terrifying
retribution that is inherent in the nature of evil. In Christian terms,
when man denies his obedience to God—then there is a price to
pay. It is the law of his nature, the law of creation. And the
application of this is ethical as well as spiritual: it is as fundamental
in human relationships and in self-respect (drug-taking?) as in his
final rejection of, or acceptance of, his relationship with God.

John Wain has a further point to make. Always, he says, there
has been a sense of the need for absolution: something to objectify
and make effective our penitence.

> Men have clung always to emblems,
> to tokens of absolution from their sins.
> Once it was the scapegoat driven out, bearing
> its load of guilt under the empty sky
> until its shape was lost, merged in the scrub.
> Now we are civilised, there is no wild heath.
> Instead of the nimble scapegoat running out
> to be lost under the wild and empty sky,
> the load of guilt is packed into prison walls,
> and men file inwards through heavy doors.

> But now that image, too, is obsolete . . .[8]

[7] John Wain, 'A Song about Major Eatherly', Section 3, in *Weep
before God* (Macmillan, 1961).
[8] *Op. cit.*, Section 4.

The need for a scapegoat . . . the emblem of absolution. For John Wain and most modern writers the desire is there and a vision of the need: but the image is obsolete. The Christian affirmation is that the need is supplied, the emblem takes life, the God who tells parables *lives* them too. And in the historical facts and existential implication of the incarnation and crucifixion and resurrection we find at once, and together, the Christian answer both to this urgently-felt, historically-expressed need, and to the last of our questions on Christian identity, '*Where* am I?'

REALITIES OF TIME AND PLACE

In view of the widely-felt belief today in the absurdity of life which we looked at in Chapter 5, our sense of *location* is a vitally important one. We need to feel that time and place have a reality, that all is not nothingness. And to do this we must at once think clearly— use our minds—and trust hopefully—submit our faith. For accepting the 'Absurd' view of life involves a kind of faith in almost the same sense as Christianity. Dr Blaiklock puts this well in his commentary on Luke's Gospel:[9]

> Alternatives stand before the seeker. He must, in point of fact, take one or another path of faith. For let the one who rejects God and His Christ realise that he is not done with faith. If he pleads insufficient proof to warrant acceptance, he must equally admit that the contrary choice also lacks final proof. The last act is the committal of the life to the likelier alternative.

I am not being *more* honest in affirming the fear of nothingness than in asserting the joy of certainties. The queasiness of terror I feel at the contemplation of meaninglessness and nothingness is real. But it is no more real than the sense of security and 'groundedness' I feel when I recognize my relationship to God.

THE GOD OF THE HERE AND NOW AND THE THEN AND THERE

But this reality is not merely grounded in my own subjective reactions. It is real not merely because I feel the reality of it, but

[9] Scripture Union Bible Study Books, 1966.

because it has an objective basis. Richard Niebuhr has word to say on this in *Christ and Culture*.[1] Speaking of th standing of the Christian faith in existentialist terms, t active 'encounter' between man and God, he points must experience the direct and individual confronta Christ; but without companions, collaborators, teachers, ting witnesses 'I am at the mercy of my imaginatio Jesus Christ of *history* is an essential part of my existenti Our present moment of decision is not a non-hist without connection of future and past.

This is the root of the Christian's awareness of is not merely a God of the mystical, rejecting any the physical, the time and place, the 'planes of bei preach Him thus would be to enact the Gnosti again. He is at once the God of the above and and now, and the then and there. *Because* He int at a particular place among particular people, for all time His concern with this moment, therefore my hour and my home and my p concern. This has been so ever since He firs create man, and His intervention in the incar in the crucifixion were a re-affirmation of it:

> For our God hath blessed Creation,
>   Calling it good. I know
> That spirit with whom you blindly band
> Hath blessed destruction with his hand;
> Yet by God's death the stars shall stand
>   And the small apples grow.[2]

For this reason that view of God which while exciting and valuable in its insist man/Christ encounter, leaves something

[1] Faber and Faber, 1952.
[2] From G. K. Chesterton, *The Ballad of th*
[3] *Cf.*, *e.g.*, Professor Bultmann's insi God can have any meaning for us unless about ourselves, unless it can have so shown to affect the way we live, or the in which we live.

119

on earth is named'[4] and our final understanding of our Christian identity must be in terms of our family in God. That same Terry whom I quoted earlier, speaking in *Talking to a Stranger*, had gone home for help and found none, as she tells her brother, Alan:

ALAN: Come home.

TERRY: Not home—this—isn't my home. If I've got a home—and I'm not sure about that—'cause I don't know what the word means. If I've got a home. . . .

ALAN: Fixed residence—I think. Dwelling house.

TERRY: It isn't here.

ALAN: Household.

TERRY: It's way off—in my mind—and till I find it. . . .

ALAN: Got it! Fixed residence of family.

TERRY: This is a family?

ALAN: Isn't it?

TERRY: The outward and visible—maybe—if you don't look too closely. . . .

ALAN: It's the only one you've got.[5]

The human family had broken down. It was ineffective. Under the kind of pressure we know all too well today, it was showing the rupture and uselessness that modern sociologists are pointing out to us as making the family unit no longer viable or serviceable. But the glorious thing about the Christian affirmation is that Alan's final line is not wholly true. The clear assertion of the Christian faith is that shared acceptance of Christ's Lordship means becoming part of the 'family of God'. This is no mere good fellowship—all shake hands and sing 'Auld Lang Syne'. This is a

[4] Ephesians 3:14, 15.

[5] See Robert Frost, 'The Death of the Hired Man', *Selected Poems* (Penguin, 1955):

'Home', he mocked gently,

'Yes, what else but home?

It all depends on what you mean by home' . . .

'Home is the place where, when you have to go there,

They have to take you in.'

'I should have called it

Something you somehow haven't to deserve.'

profoundly real 'membership one of another', being the 'body of Christ', knowing a corporateness that is shaped by, empowered by, the Holy Spirit. It is not merely that Christians are interdependent, learning from each other, and sharing with each other, as in the human family pattern: though this can *never* be stressed too strongly. (We can never grow as Christians as we were meant to do without the grace of each other's fellowship.) But much more profoundly than that, our whole Christian identity is involved in this corporate-ness. Paul expounds in his letter to the Romans:

> For if many died through one man's trespass, much more have the grace of God and the free gift in the grace of that one man Jesus Christ abounded for many. . . . Then as one man's trespass led to condemnation for all men, so one man's act of righteousness leads to acquittal and life for all men.[6]

'Don't blame me, I'm not Adam', Brian Higgins said in his poem on 'The North' quoted in Chapter 3. But we have seen how increasingly men have become aware that they *are* Adam; that they are 'involved in the human race'; that the crime of one is the crime of all, that Belsen is in our blood, that all our hands are guilty. We share in each other's responsibility; we know each other's secret. We know Adam's, and we pay his price.

This is what the mid-century knows. What it does not know, what is has not dared recognize, is that, in the sense in which we are all involved in Adam, so we can all be involved in Christ. One man is guilty; and we share his guilt. But one Man, alone, was wholly, sacrificially good; and we may, through faith in Him, share His righteousness. Michael Green in *The Meaning of Salvation* puts it thus:

> Without the two-fold solidarity of God with us in Christ, and of us with Christ in God, the New Testament doctrine of justification . . . would be immoral. As it is, there is no question of 'legal fiction', for believers *are* in Christ and share His status of righteousness.[7]

That is, one Man paid Adam's price. Our price. One Man, encountering the Belsen, paid in full the debt of Belsen, made it

[6] Romans 5:15 ff.
[7] From Chapter 9 of E. M. B. Green, *The Meaning of Salvation*.

His own, and met the cost. All we have to do is accept, with a sort of shuddering that turns to wondering that turns to glorying, that we, in Him, have paid. All we have to do is accept; but that is the hardest of all. Yet if we do accept, then we take on a new identity, a family likeness; there is indwelling a Spirit which transforms, by the renewing of our minds, so that we come—at last—'in the unity of the faith and of the knowledge of the Son of God, to the measure of the stature of the fullness of Christ . . .

. . . unto a perfect man'.

INDEX

Some of the poems quoted in this book are collected in anthologies, as follows (page numbers refer to this book): pp. 83, 111, *An Anthology of Modern Verse 1940-60*, edited by E. Jennings (Methuen, 1961); pp. 38f., *The Mid Century English Poetry 1940-60*, edited by D. Wright (Penguin, 1965); pp. 7, 33, 43, 44, 105, 106, 108, *Modern Religious Verse*, selected by T. Beaumont (Studio Vista, 1966); pp. 32f., 80, *The New Poetry*, selected by A. Alvarez (Penguin, 1962).

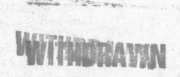